To CHANGE TO Root
TYPE CD\ and then press enter.

The Complete Idiot's Reference Card

Anatomy of a DOS Command

DOS prompt

DOS command

Switch

C:\DOS>DIR A: /P

Current directory

Parameter

Current drive

Current drive   Displays the letter of the active drive.

Current directory   Displays the path to the active directory.

DOS prompt   A message from DOS letting you know that it is waiting for a command.

DOS command   Tells DOS to perform some specific task.

Parameter   Specifies the files, the directory, or the drive with which to work.

Switch   Options you can use with a command.

alpha books

Idiot-Proof DOS Command List

You need at least DOS 4   *You need at least DOS 5*   *You need DOS 6*   *Any DOS version*

If you want to do this . . .	*Then type this . . . and press Enter*
Clear your screen	**CLS**
Find out your DOS version you're using	**VER**
Get help	**HELP**
List files one screen at a time	**DIR /P**
List files on drive A	**DIR A: /P**
List files across the screen	**DIR /W /P**
List files alphabetically	**DIR /O**
Change to the \WORD directory	**CD \WORD**
Create a new directory	**MD C:\WORD\DOCS**
Rename a directory	**MOVE C:\OLDDIR C:\NEWDIR**
Remove a directory without files	**RD \OLD**
Remove a directory with files	**DELTREE \OLD**
Make a duplicate of CONFIG.SYS	**COPY CONFIG.SYS CONFIG.BAK**
Copy a file to a different directory	**COPY C:\MKTG\SALES.DOC C:\ACCTG**
Move a file	**COPY BUDGET.WKS C:\TAXES**
	DEL BUDGET.WKS
Move a file	**MOVE BUDGET.WKS C:\TAXES**
Rename a file	**REN OLDFILE.DOC NEWFILE.DOC**
Delete a file	**DEL OLDFILE.DOC**
Restore an accidentally deleted file	**UNDELETE IMPTFILE.DOC**
Format a disk	**FORMAT A: /V**
Format a double-density 5 1/4-inch diskette	**FORMAT A: /F:360**
Format a double-density 3 1/2-inch diskette	**FORMAT A: /F:720**
Format a previously formatted diskette	**FORMAT A: /Q**
Format a diskette unconditionally	**FORMAT A: /U**

Idiot-Proof DOS Command Guide

When you enter a DOS command, it acts on the files in the current drive or directory unless you specify otherwise by using a file path. A path consists of three parts:

The drive the file is located on followed by a colon, as in **C:**

A backslash (\) followed by the complete path to the file. Start with the parent directory, then add another backslash, and a subdirectory name if applicable. Finish up with a final backslash, as in **\PROJECTS\DOSBOOK**.

End the path name with a file name or file specification, as in **CHAPTR08.DOC**.

The completed path would look like this: **C:\PROJECTS\DOSBOOK\CHAPTR08.DOC**.

To Err Is Common

Here are a few common error messages. Don't see your error message here? Look in the back of the book.

Bad command or file name Maybe you made a typing error, or maybe the program doesn't exist.

File not found Maybe you typed wrong. Or maybe the file doesn't exist.

General failure error reading drive x There might not be a disk in the drive, or the disk might not be formatted.

Invalid parameter or **Invalid switch** You might have used the wrong parameter or switch, or added spaces in the wrong places.

Required parameter missing You left out some part of the command. Check what you typed.

alpha books

Anatomy of the DOS 6 Shell

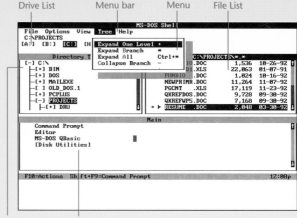

Drive List   Menu bar   Menu   File List

Directory Tree   Program List

Drive List Use these to change from drive to drive. The current drive is highlighted.

Menu bar Open a menu and select commands by clicking on them.

Menu Displays a list of commands.

File List These are the files in the current directory.

Directory Tree These are all the directories on the current drive. The current directory is highlighted.

Program List You can start a program or utility from this list.

Help-O-Rama

Here's a hodgepodge of helpful hints for common situations:

I'm done with my work, now what do I do? Always save your file, then quit or exit the program before you turn off your PC.

I'm done with this diskette, now what do I do? Make sure that the diskette light is out, then remove the diskette and place it in its paper sleeve (if the diskette has one).

My program won't start! Are you in the correct directory? Type **DIR C:*.** to see a list of the main directories on your disk. If you find the right directory, type **CD** followed by the name of the directory to change to, then try starting the program again.

I can't find my file! Don't panic; your file is probably in another directory. If you have at least DOS 5, type something like: **DIR C:\LOSTFILE.DOC /S.** (Substitute your file's name for "LOSTFILE.DOC".) If you don't have at least DOS 5, perform a directory by directory search. Change to a directory, then type **DIR /W.** Look for your file. Do you see it? If not, change to another directory by using the CD command.

Somebody help me, I deleted the wrong file! If you have at least DOS 5, change to the directory where the file was, then type something like this: **UNDELETE GOODFILE.DOC.**

You Just Gotta Have These!

If you don't do anything else today, place these two commands in your AUTOEXEC.BAT. See Chapter 16 for help.
PATH=C:\DOS   **PROMPT PG**

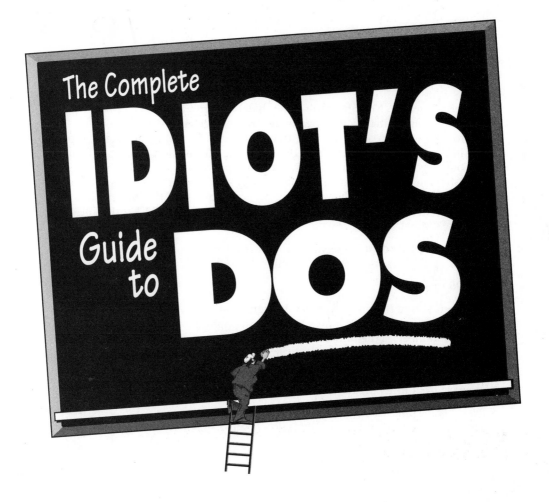

The Complete IDIOT'S Guide to DOS

by Jennifer Flynn

alpha books

A Division of Prentice Hall Computer Publishing
11711 North College Avenue, Carmel, Indiana 46032 USA

For Scott, who makes me laugh when DOS doesn't.

©1993 Alpha Books

International Standard Book Number: 1-56761-169-9
Library of Congress Catalog Card Number: 92-76075

96 95 94 93   7 6 5 4 3

Interpretation of the printing code: the rightmost number of the first series of numbers is the year of the book's printing; the rightmost number of the second series of numbers is the number of the book's printing. For example, a printing code of 93-1 shows that the first printing of the book occurred in 1993.

Screen reproductions in this book were created by means of the Collage Plus program from Inner Media, Inc., Hollis, NH.

Printed in the United States of America

Publisher   *Marie Butler-Knight*
Associate Publisher   *Lisa A. Bucki*
Managing Editor   *Elizabeth Keaffaber*
Acquisitions Manager   *Stephen R. Poland*
Development Editor   *Faithe Wempen*
Production Editor   *Annalise N. Di Paolo*
Copy Editor   *San Dee Phillips*
Cover Designer   *Scott Cook*
Designer   *Amy Peppler-Adams*
Illustrator   *Steve Vanderbosch*
Indexers   *Jeanne Clark, Joy Dean Lee*
Production Team   *Tim Cox, Mark Enochs, Tom Loveman, Michael J. Nolan, Joe Ramon, Carrie Roth, Mary Beth Wakefield, Barbara Webster, Kelli Widdifield*

Special thanks to Kelly Oliver for ensuring the technical accuracy of this book.

Contents

Before You Call the PC Doctor   **231**

A DOS Command Reference That Even
My Mother Would Love   **237**

Introduction

You are an intelligent, mature adult. You know how to balance a budget, book a one-day meeting in Chicago, and get the copier to collate (and staple!). You don't need a computer book that treats you like a child.

On the other hand, you don't need a book that assumes you are (or want to become) a PC wizard. You're a busy person with a real life beyond your computer (which you'll be glad to get back to as soon as you can get your PC to do what you need).

Why Do You Need This Book?

With so many computer books on the market, why do you need this one? Well, first off, this book won't assume that you know anything at all about how to use a computer. Every term, every instruction, is fully explained— and *in English!* (I think it's easier to climb a ladder when the first rung isn't over your head.)

This book will help you feel comfortable using DOS and your computer, while cleverly avoiding anything that could make you a PC expert. Believe me, you do not want to become THE expert on anything, especially computers. Simply open the book when you have a question or problem, read what you need to, and get back to your life.

How Do I Use This Book?

For starters, don't actually *read* this book! (At least not the whole thing.) When you need a quick answer, use the Table of Contents or the Index to find the right section. Each section is self-contained, with exactly what you need to know to solve your problem or to answer your question.

When you need to type something, it will appear like this:

TYPE THIS STUFF IN

Just type what you see and press the **Enter** key. It's as simple as that. (By the way, if you're supposed to press a particular key, that key will appear in bold, as the **Enter** key does here.)

Here are some special boxed notes that are used in this book to help you learn just what you need:

By the Way . . .
Special hints and amusing anecdotes from me.

Put It to Work
Real-life, time-saving ways you can use DOS.

Easy-to-understand definitions for every computer term let you "speak like a geek."

Skip this background fodder (technical twaddle) unless you're truly interested.

Notes and tips showing the easiest way to perform some task.

There's help when things go wrong!

Make sure to watch for the special "What's Wrong with This Picture?" sections; they highlight simple exercises that test what you've learned.

Acknowledgments

Thanks to all the great people at Alpha Books for allowing me to write a computer book for regular people and for realizing learning can be fun!

Trademarks

All terms mentioned in this book that are known to be trademarks or service marks are listed below. In addition, terms suspected of being trademarks or service marks have been appropriately capitalized. Alpha Books cannot attest to the accuracy of this information. Use of a term in this book should not be regarded as affecting the validity of any trademark or service mark.

MS-DOS is a trademark of Microsoft Corporation.

Part One
Dad Does DOS—
The Basics of Using a
Computer

My dad is a great guy—and smart, too. He can change a tire, sharpen the blades on a lawn mower without getting nicked, and figure a sales discount in his head. He once fixed the toilet with a paper clip, yet he's stumped by this thing called a computer.

The computer age crept up on some of us adults without our even knowing it. One day, we were marveling at pocket calculators the size of toasters; the next day, we were desperately trying to coax OUR OWN MONEY from automatic teller machines. Soon PCs were so fast and so cheap that everyone felt obligated to buy them (including your boss).

So maybe you're sitting there, just like my dad, with a brand-new computer that one of your kids gave you for Christmas. Relax. It's much easier to make a computer do what you want than to paper-train a puppy or coax a 2-year-old to eat peas. In this section, you'll start to learn how.

Chapter 1
The Top Ten Things You Need to Know About DOS

Just like those other "notes" you used to buy in high school to avoid reading books, here's a Jennifer's Notes version of the amazing facts you'll find in this great book. If you read nothing else in this book, for gosh sakes, read this! So what do you really need to know about DOS?

1. **You need to be able to recognize the DOS prompt.** The DOS prompt is a message from DOS letting you know that it is waiting for a command. When you type a command, it will appear next to the prompt on-screen. Typical DOS prompts include **C>** or **C:\DOS>**, and next to the prompt, you'll find the *cursor*. The cursor is a horizontal blinking line that acts like the tip of your pencil; commands that you type will appear on-screen at the cursor.

2. **You need to know what DOS version you are using**. Some commands are only included with the latest DOS version, DOS 6. To see what DOS version you have, type this:

   VER

   and press **Enter**. To learn more about the latest DOS version, see Chapter 8.

3. **You must remember to press Enter to execute a command.** Until you press Enter, nothing will happen. If you want to know more about how to enter DOS commands, see Chapter 4.

4. **You must know what a file is, and what a directory is for.** DOS stores information in *files*. Anything can be placed in a file: a

memo, a budget report, or even a graphics image (like a picture of a boat or a computer). You use *directories* like partitions to organize your files. Think of a directory as a drawer in a large file cabinet; you keep your files in whatever drawers (directories) you want. To learn more about files and directories, read Chapter 6.

5. **You need to know where you can go for help.** If you are using at least DOS version 5 (see number 2), you can get instant help on any command by typing **HELP**. For example, to get help on the COPY command, type this:

    HELP COPY

    or you can type this:

    COPY /?

    To learn more about the DOS help system, see Chapter 8.

6. **You must understand the proper care and feeding of your new pet.** Never plug anything into your computer while the computer is on. Keep drinks at a safe distance, so they don't gum up the works. Never remove a diskette while the drive light is on, and never give your PC a bath (think of it as a big cat). For more timely tips, see Chapter 3.

7. **You should know to never turn off or restart the computer while you are in a program.** You'll lose what you're working on. If you're stuck and don't know what to do, see Chapter 3.

8. **You must know the difference between the forward slash (/) and the backslash (\).** The forward slash is used to designate a *switch*, which is a part of a DOS command that overrides what it normally does. For example, if you type just

    DIR

    you'll get a listing of files in the current directory, down the screen. But if you type

    DIR /W

the files will be displayed across the screen instead of downward. The backslash is used in path names, to designate a directory, as in

C:\DOS

or to separate a directory name from a file name, as in

C:\WORD\DOCS\CHAP10.DOC.

To learn more about entering DOS commands, see Chapter 4.

9. **If you accidentally delete a file, try to undelete it as soon as you can.** If you have at least DOS version 5, you can undelete files, *but you must try not do anything on your computer until you've rescued the deleted file.*

10. **Buy the type of diskettes that match the kind of diskette drive that your PC has.** Diskettes (small plastic things that you save your work on) come in many sizes and capacities. If you don't buy the right kind, they may not work, or they may be too much trouble. If you want to know more about diskettes, see Chapter 5.

I know, I know . . . so I lied, but this is too good to leave out:

11. **I don't want to rain on your parade, but there are some rather boring but important things you can do to save your work from accidental destruction.** If I just got your attention, see Chapters 14, 15, and 17—all others go to the back of the class.

Chapter 2

So You Got a Computer, Whaddya Do with It Now?

In This Chapter

- ☞ What is a computer?
- ☞ Great things you can do with a computer
- ☞ Understanding the parts of a computer
- ☞ How to use the keyboard
- ☞ How does DOS fit into the picture?
- ☞ How to tell what DOS version you are using
- ☞ How the Shell makes DOS easier to use

This chapter will explain all those "little things" that people forgot to tell you to do when using a computer. Understanding what a computer is will help you learn to communicate with it. And if you're wondering what all those keys are for, you're about to find out!

Hey, Somebody Stole My Typewriter!

One day, my mom walked into work and found her typewriter missing. In its place was this gray box, with something like a TV sitting on top of it. Did she panic? Not my mom—we're talking about a woman who raised ten kids. She'd watched Star Trek, so she knew what a computer was. She turned to the computer and said in her best Spock voice, "Computer on." Mom had entered the computer age.

Learning how to type with the computer keyboard was something of a challenge, but after she got used to it, Mom grudgingly admitted that she liked using the computer. With the computer, she could make last-minute changes (the kind her boss was fond of) to memos and reports, without using a single drop of White-out! Printing a copy of last month's budget meeting was as simple as pressing a key.

Getting Your Typewriter Back (What Is a PC?)

With a computer (called a *personal computer*, or PC for short) you can do more than just type. A PC takes information you type in, allows you to change it as many times as you like, stores that information in something called a *file*, and even prints it out. If you're doing something with a pencil, paper, or a calculator, chances are you could be doing that same task more efficiently and accurately with a computer.

Personal computer   A personal computer (or PC, for short) is small enough to fit on a desktop and is intended for use by an individual to perform daily tasks, such as typing, calculating, organizing, and filing.

File   DOS stores information in files. Think of placing papers in a file folder and you'll get the idea. Anything can be placed in a file: a memo, a budget report, or even a graphics image (such as a picture of a boat or a computer). Files you create are called *data files*. Applications (like a word processing program, with which you can type letters and reports) are made up of several files called *program files*.

Great Things You Can Do with a Computer

Find that missing two cents in your checkbook.

Balance your department's budget for this year.

Maintain an address book of sales contacts, account reps, friends, or family.

Figure your taxes.

Play games.

Write notes, reports, and the great American novel.

Play music. Write music. Put on a show!

Discover the artist in you, or use predrawn pictures to punch up your reports and impress your boss.

Organize your appointments, to-do lists, and those "gotta get 'em dones."

Great Things You Can't Do with a Computer

Keep your checkbook balance from going negative.

Eliminate the federal deficit.

Win the Publisher's Clearing House Sweepstakes.

Figure out why a 12-ounce soft drink costs 3 bucks at the movie theater, and only 50 cents out of a machine.

Taking a Look Inside a Computer

A person has many parts—including a heart that pumps blood, a brain that processes information (but not before 10 a.m.), and a stomach that changes food into energy. Like a human body, a computer also has many parts. Here's what all those parts do:

By the Way . . .

Wait a minute! Why should you care about all this stuff? You came here to learn about DOS, so where does DOS fit in? Well, DOS is in charge of everything you see listed here. If DOS was in control of your body, it would be the thing that keeps the heart pumping, the lungs breathing, and the brain thinking. DOS takes the individual parts of a computer and keeps them working *together*. But you'll learn more about DOS later. For now, let's find out what these things are for so we can turn the PC on.

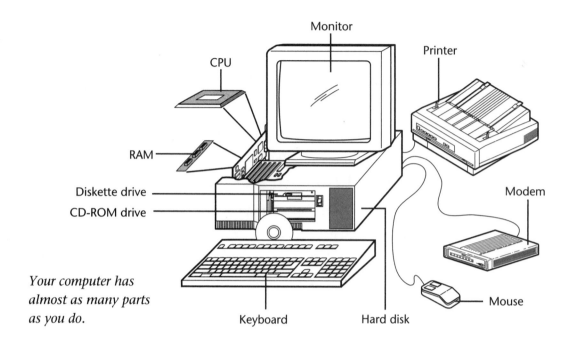

Your computer has almost as many parts as you do.

CPU   CPU stands for Central Processing Unit. The CPU is the brain of your computer. Like your brain, this is the part of the computer that "thinks" or processes information.

RAM   Stands for random-access memory. RAM is the computer's desktop, a place to work on information. When you run a program, the program moves into RAM and stays there to work. When you type in your information (also called *data*), it is stored in RAM, too. The computer forgets everything in RAM when you shut off the power, so you need to save your work onto disks (see *floppy diskettes* and *hard disk*).

Keyboard   The keyboard is the main device that you use to give the computer *input*. It has the standard keys that you find on a typewriter, plus some additional ones that you use to issue special commands.

Monitor   This is the part of the computer that looks like a TV. The computer displays its output on the monitor.

Floppy diskettes   Diskettes are small, portable, plastic storage squares (call 'em *disks* for short). Data is stored on diskettes magnetically, using a special film.

Diskette drives   The slots in the front of the computer are where you insert floppy diskettes so you can copy information onto them, or from them. Your computer may have one or two of these diskette drives.

Hard disk   Hidden inside your computer, a hard disk is like a really big diskette. A hard disk stores much more information than a floppy diskette and accesses that information much faster. Unlike a diskette, a hard disk is typically nonremovable.

Making Life Easier—Computer Accessories

Now that you've learned the basic parts of your computer system, here are a few "extras" that your computer system might include. They're not needed, but they sure do make life easier!

Mouse   The mouse provides another way to communicate with your computer. A mouse is a device that controls an arrow (a pointer) on-screen. When you move the mouse, the pointer on-screen moves. You press mouse buttons to select items on-screen. A mouse gets its name because it connects to your computer through a long "tail," or cord.

Printer   Many people have a printer connected to their computer for printing copies of data. The data that comes out of the computer is called *output*.

Modem   A modem is used to transmit or receive information through a telephone line to another computer. A *fax modem* is a special kind of modem which can (in addition to a modem's normal abilities) send and receive faxes through a telephone line.

SPEAK LIKE A GEEK

Data   A computer term for information. You enter facts and figures (data) into a computer, which then processes them and displays them in an organized manner.

Input   Input is data that you "put in" the computer. When you press a key or click a mouse button, you're giving your computer input. Data that your computer gives back to you is called *output* (because the computer "puts it out").

Disk   A round magnetic wafer on which information is stored magnetically. A *floppy disk* (diskette) can be removed from the computer, whereas a *hard disk* is usually permanent.

Output   Data (computer information) that your computer gives back to you. Output can be displayed on a computer's monitor, stored on disk, or printed on the printer. Output is the opposite of *input*.

CD-ROM drive   A popular add-on for computers. With a CD-ROM drive, your computer can play ordinary CDs (music) and special computer CDs that store complex programs or large amounts of data. For example, instead of buying a set of encyclopedias for your kids, you could buy an encyclopedia CD and not have to dust it all the time.

Surge protector/power strip   A device which protects your PC against sudden power surges. A surge protector is made up of several electrical outlets grouped together in a single unit.

Taking Care of Your Computer

You've invested a lot of money in your computer, so exercise some care. Here are some tips:

Buy a good *surge protector/power strip* to prevent damage from power surges.

Allow proper ventilation so the computer doesn't get hot.

Don't get caught by the Pepsi generation; keep liquids away from the work area. If something does spill on your keyboard, don't attempt to clean it; leave that to a PC doctor.

Don't smoke around your computer; smoke will damage the computer's sensitive parts.

Dust it once in a while. Computers collect more dust than a rag full of Pledge! Use a clean, dry cloth—no chemicals.

Playing with a Full Keyboard

If you've ever used a typewriter, you'll notice that the computer keyboard is similar, but different. Don't let all those keys intimidate you—the keyboard is easy to use when you learn the functions of the keys. Understanding the keyboard will be worth your while, since some of the special keys let you work faster in DOS.

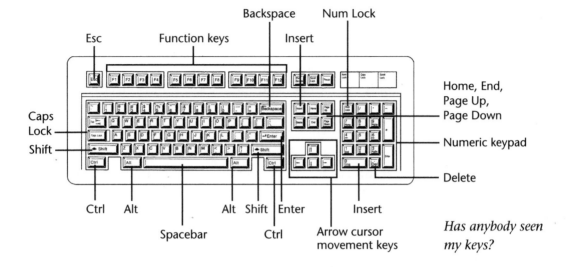

Here are the functions of some of the keys that are not so obvious:

Enter   THIS IS THE MOST IMPORTANT KEY ON YOUR KEYBOARD! DOS cannot carry out any command you type until you execute it by pressing this key.

By the Way . . .

The Enter key is something that computer manufacturers like to hide. The Enter key is often marked by a bent arrow pointing to the left, and sometimes by the word Return.

Esc   Called the Escape key, this key allows you to cancel DOS commands or to back out of an operation.

Function keys   Some programs assign a special purpose to these keys (called the F keys because they all begin with an F). DOS has a purpose for some of them, which you'll learn about later.

Shift   Used just like a typewriter to type capital letters and special characters, such as #$%?>. Sometimes used with other keys to issue commands in certain programs.

Alt and Ctrl   The Alt and Ctrl keys are used like the Shift key; press them with another key to issue commands in certain programs.

Caps Lock   This locks on capital letters. But unlike a typewriter, you will not get ! when you press the 1 key (even with the Caps Lock on). To get !, you must press the Shift key and 1 at the same time—likewise with @, #, and other special characters.

Spacebar   Just like a typewriter, this inserts spaces. You insert spaces between parts of a DOS command.

Backspace   Press this key to erase the letter or number to the left of the *cursor*. Use the Backspace key to erase all or part of a DOS command.

Cursor   The blinking box or underline that marks the place where characters will be inserted.

Arrow or cursor movement keys   These keys will make the cursor move in the direction of the arrow.

Insert or Ins   This key has a limited use in DOS, but many applications (especially word processors) use this key as a toggle between Insert mode (where existing type moves over to make room for new text) and Overstrike or Overtype mode (where new characters replace existing ones).

Delete or Del   Deletes the character at the cursor.

Home, End, Page Up, Page Down   These keys have limited use in DOS, but in most programs, Home moves the cursor to the beginning of a line; End moves the cursor to the end of a line; Page Down displays the next page of the text on-screen; and Page Up displays the previous page.

What Is DOS?

DOS (pronounced "DAHS," not "DOSE") is your **D**isk **O**perating **S**ystem. DOS is the captain, the head honcho, the big kahoona. DOS controls what your computer is doing at all times.

DOS interprets the commands you give your computer (like a United Nations translator) and controls the flow of information to each computer component (like a traffic cop).

DOS is *very particular* and requires you to type commands in a precise way, or else! It's not that DOS is stubborn; it just has a limited vocabulary. You have to use words it knows, and arrange them in an expected way, or DOS won't work for you. (Maybe DOS should stand for Deliberate Obvious Stupidity!)

DOS doesn't care whether you enter commands in upper- or lowercase letters, so use whichever you prefer.

Don't worry too much. If you do get an error message when entering a DOS command, you can turn to the back of the book and get immediate help.

How to Tell What DOS Version You Have

Some DOS features are available only with the latest version of DOS. To find out your DOS version, try out your first DOS command by typing

> **VER**

and pressing **Enter**. (If you need help turning on your PC, see Chapter 3. After you get the PC up and running, you can return here and try out your first command.) You should see something like this:

> **MS-DOS Version 6.00**

If it says **MS-DOS**, that means you're running Microsoft's original DOS and not some revamped version of it.

TECHNO NERD TEACHES

DOS is made by Microsoft, so its full name is MS-DOS. Microsoft sells MS-DOS to computer manufacturers who sometimes customize it to work specifically with their equipment. So you end up with PC-DOS (IBM's version), Compaq DOS, HP (Hewlett-Packard) DOS, Zenith DOS, and so on. These companies don't change how DOS works; they only "fine-tune" it to run on their computers. So have no fear—your DOS is *my* DOS!

The version number tells you how recent your version of DOS is. (To find out about the latest updates to DOS, see Chapter 8.)

If you are looking for the easiest way to work with DOS, use the DOS Shell (see Chapter 7 for more details). If you don't have a recent enough version of DOS, I recommend upgrading just so you can use the Shell.

An Easier DOS— The DOS Shell

If you have DOS version 4 or higher, you have another option for entering DOS commands— through the DOS Shell. The DOS Shell is a program which allows you to perform most of the same wonderful things you can with DOS, but without the headache of remembering exactly what to type. You simply point to files with the arrow keys or the mouse, select a command, and voilà!

The Least You Need to Know

Now that you've learned a little about computers, you can impress all your friends with these computer tidbits:

- ☞ A computer can imitate many things, such as a calculator, a typewriter, an address book, a notepad, a calendar, a piano, a sketch pad, and a game board.

- ☞ DOS runs the computer and interprets all commands.

- ☞ A PC forgets what is in memory (RAM) when you turn it off, so you must save your information on disk first.

- ☞ DOS doesn't know that you want it to do something until you type a command and press **Enter**.

- ☞ The **Esc** key is a good way to cancel a DOS command.

- ☞ DOS doesn't care if you use upper- or lowercase when entering commands.

- ☞ You can tell what DOS version you are using by using the DOS command **VER**.

- ☞ If you have DOS version 4 or higher, you can use the DOS Shell and save yourself the normal headaches of working with DOS.

Chapter 3
Gentlemen (and Ladies), Start Your PCs!

In This Chapter

- ☞ How to start your computer safely
- ☞ Restarting your computer (after the power is on)
- ☞ What is a CONFIG.SYS?
- ☞ What is an AUTOEXEC.BAT?
- ☞ Telling your computer what day it is
- ☞ Turning your computer off safely
- ☞ How to know when something is wrong

The information in this chapter will help you get your PC up and running safely. Even if you've already started your computer, this chapter will answer some questions you might still have about the whole process, such as "What were those funny numbers and other messages for?" You'll learn how to tell when something goes wrong and some quick tricks to use when it does.

Starting Your PC

To start (*boot*) your PC, you turn the power on. Sounds easy, but it may not be that simple. It seems that a number of computer manufacturers got together and decided on the most obscure places to hide the ON switch.

When trying to locate the power switch, follow these clues:

Clue #1: Look for something orange.

Clue #2: Look on the right side or the front or the back of the PC. But don't expect to find the familiar words ON and OFF—instead you'll probably find the secret codes I and 0.

Clue #3: I means ON and 0 means OFF!

What Happens When You Turn Your Computer On

How can you tell if the PC is working okay? Well, computers go through a self check (called POST, or power on self test) when they start. During POST, each system component is checked to verify that it is connected properly to the main system. Numbers flash on-screen as the memory (RAM) is counted and checked. Some other messages may appear; they come from the computer system itself, or from two special files: the CONFIG.SYS and the AUTOEXEC.BAT. You'll learn about them later in this chapter.

What If Nothing Happens?

If you find the power switch and turn it on but nothing happens, check these things:

Is the system unit plugged in?

Is the monitor plugged in and connected to the system unit?

Are any of the connections loose, or have any of the plugs fallen out?

If the cords are plugged into a surge protector/power strip, is it turned on? (Power strips usually have their own on/off switches.)

Does the outlet have power? (Pretty obvious, but as a quick check, plug a lamp into the same outlet. It could be illuminating.)

If you get the error message **Non-system disk or disk error. Replace and strike any key when ready**, don't panic. You may simply have left a diskette in drive A. (This is the left or top diskette drive.) Remove it and reboot (press **Ctrl**, **Alt**, and **Delete** at the same time) to continue. If that doesn't work, there may be a problem with your hard drive. Refer to the back of the book for more help.

Don't Worry About Your CONFIG.SYS Unless You Like Having It Your Way

TECHNO NERD TEACHES

Why wouldn't you just "strike any key" to continue, as DOS tells you to do? Well, you could, and it would probably be fine. But if that diskette in your drive A had a computer virus on it, that virus could be passed to your system if you continued by pressing a key. For maximum safety, use **Ctrl+Alt+Delete** instead. You'll learn more about viruses in Chapter 17.

CONFIG.SYS is a special file which is used by DOS at startup. The CONFIG.SYS is a "DOS tailor" which changes the default settings (*CONFIGuration*) of your computer so that it can work more efficiently for your specific needs. You use a tailor so your clothes fit more comfortably, so why not use CONFIG.SYS so your PC runs your programs more efficiently?

CONFIG.SYS is created when you first install DOS (DOS versions 5 and above) and can be modified easily whenever you like, or whenever a new application requires it. (Use the DOS Editor described in Chapter 16.)

If you're a beginner and you find yourself without a CONFIG.SYS for one reason or another, buy a box of Ho Ho's and bribe a PC guru to create the missing CONFIG.SYS for you.

What Kind of Commands Would You Want in Your CONFIG.SYS?

In your CONFIG.SYS file, you want commands that

Change the number of files that a program can open at one time.

Change the number of recently opened files that are in memory.

Allow your computer to use memory more efficiently.

Run special programs called *device drivers*.

Device drivers   Special programs (with names that usually end with .DRV or .SYS) that tell your computer how to communicate with certain devices, such as a mouse.

AUTOEXEC.BAT   A special file that contains commands which are automatically executed when your computer is booted.

Prompt   The prompt is a message from DOS letting you know that it is waiting for a command. When you type a command, it will appear next to the prompt on-screen. Typical DOS prompts include **C>** or **C:\DOS>**.

What Is an AUTOEXEC.BAT? (Who's Running This Thing?)

Some things may happen automatically when you start your computer. A menu may be displayed, a program may run, or the default startup procedure may begin, which will

Display the current date and ask for confirmation.

Display the current time and ask for confirmation.

Display a *prompt*, then wait for you to tell it to do something.

If anything else happens when you start your PC—if additional startup commands are issued automatically—your computer's not possessed; it's being controlled by a file called AUTOEXEC.BAT.

AUTOEXEC.BAT is a file that, like the CONFIG.SYS, is created when you first install DOS (DOS 5 and above). In the file is a series of commands that you want *AUTO*matically *EXEC*uted (carried out) when the computer is started. If you need to, grab two boxes of Ho Ho's, and while that PC guru is creating your CONFIG.SYS, have her create an AUTOEXEC.BAT, too.

What Kind of Commands Will You Want in Your AUTOEXEC.BAT?

Commands that tell the computer to

Search for files when it can't find them. (See Chapter 4 for more information on the PATH command.)

Change the default prompt from **C>** to something different. (See Chapter 6 for more on the PROMPT command.)

Start a favorite menu program or DOS shell.

Start some other program that you use first thing every day.

The .BAT in AUTOEXEC.BAT tells you it's a batch file, which is a special file that contains a number of commands. (The commands are batched together in one file, hence the name.) Batch files are handy for all sorts of things. For example, the steps involved in moving several files from one place to another can be quite involved. You can put these commands in a batch file and run that batch file whenever you need to move files.

Does Your Computer Really Know What Time It Is?

Not all computers have been set up to run DOS in exactly the same way. Some computers will display a plain prompt upon starting up or maybe a colorful menu. Some systems, during the process of starting, may ask you to enter the current date and time.

If at sometime during startup, your PC stops to display the message

Current date is Tue 01-01-1980
Enter new date (mm-dd-yy):

take a careful look at the date (it may already be correct). If it is not correct (if it's only 13 years off, like our example), then enter the correct date in the format mm-dd-yy (*month-day-year*, entering a two-digit number for each). For example, if the date is March 3, 1993, type **03-03-93** and press **Enter**.

TECHNO NERD TEACHES

What's the difference between CONFIG.SYS and AUTOEXEC.BAT (and why can't I remember the difference)? It seems stupid that DOS has two files that seem to do the same thing—customize what happens when you start your computer.

Actually, DOS is not being redundant; each file serves a specific purpose that complements but doesn't repeat the other. CONFIG.SYS contains commands that cannot be run at the DOS prompt— they can only work within CONFIG.SYS. These commands change the way that DOS works, so the commands that go into the CONFIG.SYS must be run at a certain point during startup. AUTOEXEC.BAT commands can be executed anytime, not just at startup.

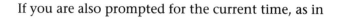

If you are also prompted for the current time, as in

Current time is 14:21:03.10
Enter new time:

then enter the correct time. Use military time, which means that 3 p.m. is really 15:00. I never bother to enter the seconds, or tenths of a second. For example, if the time is 2:30 in the afternoon, type **14:30** (**14**, **colon**, **30**) and press **Enter**. If the date and time shown are already correct, just press **Enter**.

TECHNO NERD TEACHES

Where do most computers get the default date of January 1, 1980? Well, that's pretty much when the first version of DOS was invented, so to a personal computer, nothing exists before that date. As a matter of fact, you can't enter a date prior to January 1, 1980, because to the computer, that wouldn't make sense. You also can't enter any illogical date (such as February 31st).

Should You Really Care (About the Date)?

Should you care if your computer thinks it's January 1st, 1980? Yes! Because when you save your work or make changes, the computer remembers the date and time when that was done. By keeping your computer up-to-date, you can figure out when John last updated the department budget report. Or if you have copies of the same document on several diskettes, you can figure out which is the most recent one.

If Your Computer Doesn't Ask You for a Date

If you aren't prompted for the date and time, or if the date and time shown by the computer are correct, it means that the computer already knows what day it is. How? Most computers come with a built-in clock, which keeps them updated as to the current date and time.

This internal clock runs all the time, even when the power is off, just like the clock in your car. Once in a while, the battery that runs that clock will go dead, and it will need to be replaced. It won't happen for years, but when it does, bully someone into changing it for you.

You should check the computer's date and time occasionally, because computer clocks sometimes get off track. To verify the current date (or to enter a new one), type

DATE

and press **Enter**. Your PC displays the current date and asks if you want to change it. If you want to change it, enter the new date in the format *mm-dd-yy*, as described previously. If you don't want to change it, just press **Enter**.

The TIME command works the same way. Type

TIME

and press **Enter**. Enter the new time in the format *hh:mm* (using military time) as described earlier. If the time is correct, simply press **Enter**.

Some people put the DATE and TIME commands in their AUTOEXEC.BAT just to verify that the system clock is correct.

Turning Off Your Computer—Safely

When it's time to go home, reach for the old power switch and turn the PC off—*not!*

Before you turn off your PC, make sure that you have saved your work and exited the program you were using. See Chapter 20 for help.

By the Way . . .

Shutting Down for the Night (Should You or Shouldn't You?) Should you turn off your computer at night or leave it on all the time? Even Judge Wapner can't decide:

The prosecution argues that by leaving your PC on all the time, you avoid stressing your computer by supplying it with a constant flow of energy (and not surges). The temperature of the computer parts also remains constant.

continues

continued

The defense argues that leaving a computer on all the time wastes energy and increases the chances of damage by an unexpected power surge. Also, a computer needs to be restarted (booted) from time to time.

The decision? Split down the middle. Roughly 50% of all computer users turn their computers off at the end of the day, and the other 50% leave them on. I turn my computer off every day (probably because of my childhood—"Do you think we own stock in the electric company?"), and I'm happy to report, no damages. What should you do? Do whatever feels best for your situation.

Crash Landings—Shutting Down When You Have a Problem

You may find that you need to reset your computer during the working day. You'll be in a program, and the computer may suddenly "pack its bags and fly south." (When I get really frustrated, I buy a ticket and join it in Florida.) You might see a bunch of weird characters on your screen, or your computer might simply stop doing anything whatsoever.

The reasons will vary—a sudden power surge or a glitch in the hard drive. Maybe some poorly written program has confused DOS, or maybe two of your programs don't get along with each other. At any rate, it's not your fault.

How often does this happen? Maybe never. But if it does, you must restart the computer to get it to respond. Restarting the computer is called *rebooting*. To reboot, press and hold the **Ctrl** and **Alt** keys while you press the **Delete** key. (This sequence is typically shown as **Ctrl+Alt+Delete**.)

Don't reboot a computer unless you have to, because you'll lose any unsaved work. If the computer starts acting funny, try pressing **Esc**. (If you don't know how to tell, see my sure signs that something's wrong in the next section.) If that doesn't work, press and hold the **Ctrl** key while pressing the key with Break written on the front edge (this is usually the Pause key). Pressing Ctrl+Break tells DOS to stop what it's doing, and can sometimes bring a computer out of its funk. If all else fails, you may need to reboot.

Rebooting causes your PC to clear out any "goop" in memory and start over. If your system is really locked up, you may have to perform a *cold boot*, which means you simply turn the computer off, wait a few seconds, and then turn it back on again.

You Should Reboot When . . . (Jennifer's Sure Signs That Something's Wrong)

Pick a key, any key.   You press one key (such as G) and you get something else (such as &F%^&*90/?).

Lights on, but nobody's home.   You press a key and you get no response. (Kinda like asking your boss for a $100,000 raise—no response.)

Cursor, cursor, who's got the cursor?   You press an arrow key and the cursor goes zipping in the opposite direction.

Did you hear anything?   The computer starts making more noises than a 2-year-old in church. Be sure to listen for odd beeps and grinding noises—anything that seems out of the ordinary.

SPEAK LIKE A GEEK

Rebooting   The process of restarting a computer that is already on. Press **Ctrl**, **Alt**, and **Delete** at the same time to reboot. Also known as *warm booting*.

Warm booting   Same as rebooting.

Cold booting   Same thing as booting; the process of starting a computer by turning the power on.

The Least You Need to Know

Well, congratulations graduate! Others may quake in fear, but not you—because now you know

☞ How to start your PC safely and without fear. (Remember to look for the power switch on the right side, on the front, or on the back.)

☞ If you get the message **Non-system disk or disk error**, you should look for a diskette in drive A (the left or topmost diskette drive). Remove it and press **Ctrl+Alt+Del** to restart.

☞ AUTOEXEC.BAT and CONFIG.SYS are special files that issue commands at startup. You can use them to customize your PC's operations.

☞ How to keep your PC up-to-date and on time by using the DOS commands DATE and TIME.

☞ How to turn your computer off safely. If you are using a program, use the command to save your information before you power down.

☞ What to do if your computer acts up, and how to tell if you have trouble. Try pressing **Esc** or **Ctrl+Break**. If that doesn't work, try rebooting by pressing **Ctrl+Alt+Delete**.

Chapter 4
May DOS Take Your Order, Please?

In This Chapter

- Understanding the DOS prompt
- How to change the active drive
- How to enter a DOS command
- What to do when error messages appear
- Setting up a path so you can use all of the DOS commands
- How to repeat commands without retyping them
- Internal versus external commands

In this chapter, you will learn the trick of entering DOS commands correctly. If you've ever been frustrated with DOS, or if you're wondering why the computer doesn't do what you want it to do, this chapter is for you.

That DOS Prompt "Drives" Me Crazy!

You enter commands by typing them at the DOS prompt. The DOS prompt is usually some letter, followed by a greater-than sign, as in

C>

Sometimes you may see other letters, such as A, B, or D. The letter you see represents the disk drive you are working on. The letter C refers to the hard drive, and the letters A and B refer to diskette drives. (A is the left or

If you have DOS version 4 or higher, you have another option for entering DOS commands—the DOS Shell. With the DOS Shell, you can do all of the same wonderful things you can do with DOS, but without using the DOS prompt. You simply point to things with the arrow keys or with the mouse, select a command, and *voilà!* If you are looking for the easiest way to work with DOS, use the DOS Shell (see Chapter 7 for more details).

Directory Because hard disks can store thousands of files, you need a way to place related files together on the drive. If you picture your disk as a filing cabinet, then directories are like file drawers. Keeping files in separate directories (drawers) makes it easier to locate and work with related files. You'll learn more about them in Chapter 6.

topmost diskette drive, B is the right or bottom-most drive.) If you are working from a diskette drive, you may see this prompt:

A>

Additional letters such as D, E, and so on refer to additional hard drives (if any).

Sometimes, you may see a longer DOS prompt, such as

C:\DOS>

This type of prompt tells you not only what drive you're working with, but what *directory*. This prompt is telling you that you are working with drive C and the directory DOS.

Putting DOS into Drive

As you just saw, the prompt tells which drive is active. To work with a disk drive, you must activate it (change to it). For example, if you want to work with files that are stored on a diskette you've inserted into drive A, you must change to that drive.

To change to a drive, enter the drive letter, followed by a colon (:). To change to drive A, type

A:

and press **Enter**. Your prompt will look something like this

A>

To change back to drive C (the hard disk drive), type

> C:

and press **Enter**. Your prompt will change to something like

> C>

What Can Go Wrong When You're Changing Drives

Be sure to watch these things when changing drives:

Make sure to include a colon (:) and not a semicolon (;). To change drives, type the drive letter, followed by a colon.

When changing to a diskette drive, make sure there is a diskette in the drive before pressing Enter. If there is no diskette in the drive, you will get the error **Not ready reading drive *x*. Abort, Retry, Fail?** Place the diskette in the drive and press **R** for Retry.

Make sure that the diskette is formatted. You will get this error message if the diskette is not *formatted*: **General failure error reading drive *x*. Abort, Retry, Fail?** Press **F** for Fail, and then format the disk using the instructions in Chapter 13.

Do not remove a diskette until you have changed to a different drive. Don't get fancy and remove the diskette too soon, or you may see the message **Current drive is no longer valid>**. Type the drive letter you want to change to, and press **Enter**.

Don't enter a drive letter that does not exist. If you do not have a drive Q, but you type Q:, you will get the error **Invalid drive specification**. Simply type the command again, this time with a valid drive letter.

SPEAK LIKE A GEEK

Formatting A process that prepares a diskette for use. Formatting creates invisible *tracks* (circles) and *sectors* (pie-shaped wedges) on the surface of the diskette so that data can be stored in known locations. A diskette is usually formatted only once. Some diskettes can be purchased preformatted.

How to Enter a DOS Command

Entering a DOS command is easy if you know exactly what to type (well, pretty easy, as long as you don't try to type with more than one finger). Simply type the command, and press **Enter**.

For example, to find out what day your PC thinks it is, type **DATE** and press **Enter**. In this book, the command will look like this:

DATE

By the Way . . .

Make sure you press **Enter** after each command. "Enter" is the (pardon my pun) *key* word here. Nothing happens until you press that magic key.

Lions, Tigers, and Bears: What to Watch Out for When Entering Commands

Here are some pointers for typing DOS commands:

Capital letters   Actually, this just doesn't matter. Use caps or don't; DOS gives all characters equal rights. Most computer books (including this one) show DOS commands in capital letters as in **TIME**. But if you want to type **time** instead, don't let 'em change your mind.

Spaces   *This is the number one thing that people do wrong when entering DOS commands.* DOS and its use of spaces (when to put them in, when to leave them out) is darn confusing. Read on . . .

Much Ado About Spaces

How can you tell when to enter a space? Before I can answer that question, you have to understand a little bit more about DOS commands and their structure. Our guest star for this explanation is the DIR command, which is used to list the files in a directory.

A DOS command is made up of three parts:

The command itself   For example, the DIR command.

Applicable parameters   Parameters tell the command the files, the directories, or the drives to work with. For example, you can type DIR HARD2FND.DOC to list a specific file.

Applicable switches   Switches are options you can use with a command. Switches are always preceded by a forward slash (/). For example, the DIR command has a switch (/P for pause) that lists enough files to fill a screen, and then pauses until you're ready to see more files.

Each part of a DOS command is separated by a single space. Don't add spaces anywhere else.

What's Wrong with This Picture?

Let's practice what we know about DOS spaces. The DIR command has another switch (/W for wide), which tells it to list files in several columns going across the screen, instead of one column going down. Using what you just learned about spaces, here's the six-million-dollar question: How should you type this command?

DIR \W

DIR /W

DIR   /W

LIST THOSE DARN FILES

The six-million-dollar answer is

DIR /W

To Err Is Common: What to Do If You Type a Mistake

If you type a mistake before you press Enter, try one of these:

Press the Backspace key   Back up and erase the incorrect characters and retype them.

Insert or delete characters   Using the arrow keys, move the blinking cursor to the place where you want to insert a character. Once you have the cursor positioned, press any character, and it will be inserted at that spot. To delete an extra character, press **Delete** or **Del**.

Press the Esc key   This will erase the entire line and let you start over. On most computers, when you press Esc, you will see a backslash (/), and the cursor will move down one line. Type your command there. (If you feel nervous about typing a command without the DOS prompt, press **Enter** after pressing **Esc**, and Dorothy, you're back in Kansas.)

TECHNO NERD TEACHES

Pressing the **Ctrl** key produces the character, ^. So if you press **Ctrl+C**, you will see ^C on your monitor. Likewise, if you were to press **Ctrl+D**, you would see ^D, and so on.

Press Ctrl+Break   Hold down the **Ctrl** key while you press the **Break** key. It's the DOS equivalent of "Stop this nonsense or go to your room!" It works like Esc but will return you to a nice friendly DOS prompt. You can also cancel some commands with **Ctrl+Break** after they've started running. If you can't find the Break key, use **Ctrl+C** instead.

If you pressed Enter but got an error message because you mistyped the command, repeat the command by pressing **F3**. Then use the arrow keys to position the cursor where you'd like to insert or delete characters.

The Most Common Error Messages After Pressing Enter

If you get any errors after typing a DOS command, it's probably one of these (if not, refer to the "HELP! What Does This Error Message Mean, and What Can I Do About It?" section at the end of this book for a more complete listing of error messages):

Bad command or file name   If you get this error, it could be caused by one of three things:

> *Mistyped command*   Check to make sure that you didn't misspell the command or insert extra spaces.

> *External command*   Some DOS commands are available at every prompt, while others aren't. See "Setting Up a PATH for DOS to Follow" in this chapter.

> *Missing program*   If you get this error after entering a command to start a program, that program either doesn't exist anymore or is not in this directory. (Remember that a directory is like a file drawer.) See Chapter 20 for help locating your program.

File not found   If you get this error, it could be one of two things:

> *Mistyped file name*   Check to make sure that any file names you typed are valid.

> *File does not exist*   There's a possibility that the file you are looking for is not in the current directory, or the file does not exist. Try a different directory.

Invalid parameter or invalid switch   This could be the result of several things:

> *You used a parameter or switch that is invalid for this command.*   Check this book and verify what you typed.

> *You entered a space between the forward slash and the letter.*   If you want to enter a command with a switch, as in DIR /W, do not add an extra space between the slash and the W as in DIR / W.

> *You used a slash that points the wrong direction.*   Forward slashes (/) are for switches; backward slashes (\) precede directory names or stand for the root directory.

The installation program for DOS 5 or higher uses AUTOEXEC.BAT to set up a path to DOS, so you may already have a path. To find out, type **PATH** and press **Enter**. If DOS doesn't reply **No Path**, it'll show the existing one.

Required parameter missing   You left out some part of the command. Check this book and verify what you typed.

Setting Up a PATH for DOS to Follow

There are two types of DOS commands: *internal* and *external*. Internal DOS commands are always available (if you're dying to know the full story, read the "Techno Nerd Teaches" in this section). External DOS commands are not available unless

☞ You are in the DOS directory. (How do you get there? Read Chapter 6 to find out.)

OR

☞ You have set up a path for DOS to use to find the external DOS commands. (How do you set up a path? Read on . . .)

To make all DOS commands available (both internal and external), set up a DOS path. A DOS path is a listing of directories that DOS should check before it gives you a **Bad command or file name** message, meaning it can't find the command.

If you don't have a path, or if your path doesn't contain the DOS directory (C:\DOS), you need to set up a path so you can use the external DOS commands. Type

PATH=C:\DOS

This translates as "Set up a search path to drive C, to a directory called \DOS." That's it. Now your external DOS commands are available regardless of which directory you are in.

Okay, I lied. When you restart your computer, you're going to have this same problem again. To avoid ever thinking about this (ever, ever, ever), bribe a friend (I know, this book is costing you a fortune in Ho Ho's, but it's worth it) to add the PATH command to your AUTOEXEC.BAT so that the PATH command is automatically executed when you start up your computer. If you want to try editing the AUTOEXEC.BAT yourself, see Chapter 16 for instructions.

Repeating Yourself

If you are issuing the same command over and over again, you may find that typing it becomes tedious. For example, if you're examining the contents of one diskette after another, you might be typing the following command repeatedly:

DIR A:

The A: tells the DIR command to list the files on the diskette in drive A (more about drives in Chapter 5).

Instead of retyping the command every time you insert a different diskette in A, simply press **F3**. You'll see the command redisplayed:

DIR A:

Press **Enter** to execute the command, and you're on your way!

TECHNO NERD TEACHES

Certain DOS commands are called *internal* because they are loaded into memory (and are available to use) as soon as you turn on your PC. Think of internal commands as being "built in." Unlike internal commands, *external* commands reside as files in the DOS directory. They are not available until you load them into memory (by typing their name and pressing **Enter**). Like a program, external commands cannot be loaded into memory if DOS can't locate them. By setting up a path to \DOS, you are helping DOS find the external commands stored there.

The Least You Need to Know

When you say "Jump!", DOS will say "How high?" if you remember these things when entering commands:

☞ A DOS prompt tells you what drive you are using (by displaying the drive letter). Some DOS prompts may also tell you what directory you are using.

☞ Drive C is your hard disk, and drives A and B are diskette drives. Other drive letters are additional hard disks.

☞ You can change from one drive to another by typing the drive letter followed by a colon.

☞ There are three parts to a DOS command: the command itself, available parameters (directories or file names), and available switches. Switches are identified with a / followed by a letter, as in /P.

☞ Entering a DOS command can be tricky unless you remember to type only one space between the parts of a DOS command and never to use a period, except in file names.

☞ Setting up a DOS path by typing **PATH=C:\DOS** will make all DOS commands available.

Chapter 5
Becoming a Disk(ette) Jockey

In This Chapter

☛ How to maintain your hard disk in good working order

☛ How to choose the right diskette for your PC

☛ How to insert a diskette into its drive

☛ How to protect diskettes from damage

Disks and diskettes store your computer data magnetically. This chapter will show you how to "treat them right" so your data is always there when you need it. Your PC uses two different types of disks:

A *hard disk* (hidden inside the computer) that is used to store large amounts of data.

Floppy disks (diskettes) that are used to store smaller amounts of data.

See Disks Play. Play, Disks, Play

A hard disk is one of the most important parts of your computer, because it holds your programs and most of your data. Follow these tips to keep it healthy and strong:

☛ Don't let your hard disk get too hot. Make sure that the system unit (CPU) is placed in a well-ventilated spot, several inches from any wall.

SPEAK LIKE A GEEK

CMOS   Pronounced "SEA-moss." CMOS is an electronic device (usually battery operated) that stores information about your computer. Information stored in CMOS includes the current date and time (if your computer is equipped with a clock) and the number and type of disk drives your computer has. If the information in CMOS is damaged by battery failure or a system glitch, you may not be able to use the hard drive, and information may mysteriously disappear from your disk. Some utility programs, such as PC Tools, provide a way to restore the lost or damaged CMOS information and allow you to test the CMOS battery.

☛ Putting your CPU on its side is popular, but it might lead to problems if the disk has been used in the horizontal position for some time (think of trying to turn a phonograph on its side). If you want a vertical computer, buy one that's built that way (they're called towers).

☛ Always maintain a current backup (copy) of your files (see Chapter 14) in case something happens to your hard disk.

☛ If you're running out of space on your hard disk for new files, a disk compression program, (like DoubleSpace) will help (see Chapter 18).

☛ Hard disks come in different types. The kind of hard disk your system uses is stored in something called CMOS. Making a copy of this CMOS data is very important; get a guru to help you.

A Brief Disk-cussion About Diskettes

Diskettes really aren't that hard to understand, but you need to know some of the factors that go into selecting the right diskettes for your system, such as size and density.

What Size Is Right?

Diskettes come in two sizes: 5 1/4-inch and 3 1/2-inch. You buy the diskette that fits your diskette drive.

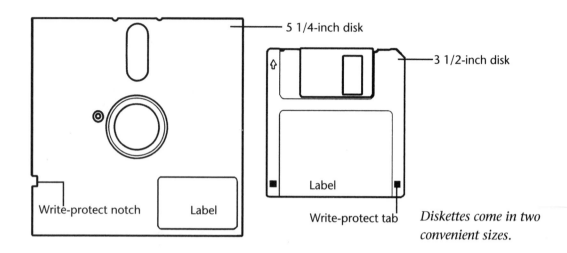

Diskettes come in two convenient sizes.

By the Way . . .

Size does not have anything to do with the amount of data a diskette can hold. In fact, the 3 1/2-inch diskettes can hold more than the 5 1/4-inch diskettes! Size is only a measure of the physical size of the plastic part.

Feeling a Bit Dense About Diskettes?

Each diskette size comes in two densities. The *density* of a diskette refers to how closely data can be packed onto the disk. A diskette that's more dense than another diskette holds more data. Imagine one phonograph record with 100 grooves, and a second record (the same size diameter) with 200 grooves. On the latter, the grooves are closer together, so more music fits on the record.

The two most common densities are *high density* and *double density*. The exact capacity depends on the diskette size, but a high-density diskette holds at least twice as much data as a double-density diskette of the same size.

Diskette Capacity—Fill It Up!

The amount of data a diskette can hold is called its *capacity*. Capacity is determined by a combination of the diskette's size and density. Diskette capacity is measured in *bytes*. A byte is the amount of space it takes for a computer to store one character, such as the letter Q. A *kilobyte* is 1,024 bytes. A *megabyte* is about 1,048,576 bytes—about 1,000 kilobytes. Kilobytes are abbreviated as K, and megabytes as MB.

Size...	Plus Density...	Equals Capacity
5 1/4-inch	Double	360K (about 360,000 bytes)
5 1/4-inch	High	1.2MB (about 1,200,000 bytes)
3 1/2-inch	Double	720K (about 720,000 bytes)
3 1/2-inch	High	1.44MB (about 1,440,000 bytes)

Choosing the Right Diskette for Your System

Obviously, you have to use the right size of diskettes in your drive, or the disk won't fit. But you must also use the right density. If your PC has a double-density 5 1/4-inch drive, you must use 5 1/4-inch double-density diskettes. So, when buying diskettes, match the diskette drive's *size* and *density*. Check your owner's manual to find out what kind of diskettes your diskette drive uses.

If you have a high-density drive, you can use either density diskette: high or double. But you can run into problems that way, so I wouldn't use anything other than a high-density diskette in a high-density drive.

By the Way . . .

The first time I went to buy diskettes, it seemed that the store was full of them! Different sizes and types (not to mention formatted and unformatted). I had a hard time figuring out which ones to buy. Look for these abbreviations:

DD	Double density.
HD	High density.
2D	Double density.
4D	Quad density, an old term for double density.
ED	Extended density. Avoid these unless you have a special extended-density drive (if you're not sure, you don't).
DS	Double sided. This is the norm because most diskette drives write data to both sides of a diskette.
SS	Single sided. These diskettes are designed for older PCs that could write data to only one side of a diskette. (They're actually double-sided, but have only been tested on one side.)

Changing Diskettes

To place a diskette in a drive, hold the disk so that your thumb covers the label, with the label pointing up (or to the left, if your drive is vertically mounted).

- ☞ 3 1/2-inch diskette—Push the diskette into the drive, metal-covered area first, until you hear a soft click.

- ☞ 5 1/4-inch diskette—Push the diskette into the drive, exposed area first (label up or to the left). Then close the drive door by pulling the lever across the slot or pressing the button.

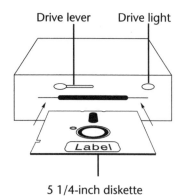

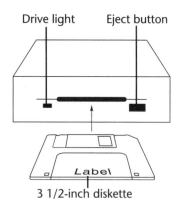

Placing a diskette in its drive.

5 1/4-inch diskette   3 1/2-inch diskette

To eject (remove) a diskette:

☞ 5 1/4-inch diskette—Open the drive door by pulling the lever up.

☞ 3 1/2-inch diskette—Press the eject button.

By the Way . . .

If a 3 1/2-inch diskette gets stuck, I push it back into the drive, and the spring inside usually bounces it back out. On a 5 1/4-inch drive, pulling the lever down and then back up usually works.

Care and Treatment of Diskettes

Here are some easy guidelines:

Removal Don't remove a diskette from its drive while the drive light is on. It could damage both the drive and the diskette.

Fingers When handling a diskette, don't touch any exposed area—you'll damage the magnetic film inside the diskette.

Heat Keep diskettes away from heat sources (such as the top of your monitor or the inside of a car on a hot day).

Magnets   Since data is stored on diskettes magnetically, keep them away from any magnetic source (like your telephone or your modem, or even your CPU).

Labeling   If you use 5 1/4-inch diskettes, complete your labels *before* placing them on the diskettes. If you have to write on a label that is already on the diskette, use a soft-tipped pen.

Storage   If you use 5 1/4-inch diskettes, place them back in their paper envelopes when not in use.

Remove the diskette from the drive when you're finished with it. If you start the computer with a disk in drive A, you may get an error message: **Non-system disk or disk error. Replace and strike any key when ready.** If that happens, remove the diskette and press **CTRL+ALT+DEL**.

The Least You Need to Know

Dealing with DOS is just another day at the races for a "disk" jockey who remembers these basic rules:

☞ Always maintain a current backup (copy) of the files on your hard disk, in case something happens.

☞ Disk compression utilities like the ones you'll read about in Chapter 18 will help you put more files on your hard disk.

☞ Diskettes come in two sizes (5 1/4-inch and 3 1/2-inch) and two densities (double and high). Density refers to how closely information is placed on the diskette.

☞ To protect diskettes, remove them from the drive when not in use. Keep diskettes away from magnets, heat, and your fingers.

Chapter 6

Using
(and Sometimes Losing)
Files and Directories

In This Chapter

- ☞ What are files?
- ☞ Naming files
- ☞ What are directories?
- ☞ Naming directories
- ☞ Changing the system prompt

When working with DOS, you use disks, files, and directories. You'll find yourself referring to this chapter (and the previous one) again and again, because it's about the things you'll use every day.

What Are Files?

Hard disks and diskettes are used to store your data. You store data in *files*, which you can think of as tiny books. If you write a memo about the copier, you might save it in a file called COPIER. If you create an analysis of shipping costs, you might save it in a file called SHIPPING. Each file you create has its own name (just as books have their own names).

File   DOS stores information in files. A file can be anything: a memo, a budget report, or even a graphics image (like a picture of a boat or a computer). Files you create are called *data files*. Applications (like a word processing program that you can type letters and reports with) are composed of several files called *program files*.

The extension of a file can tell you a lot about what type of file it is. Most word processors use a .DOC extension. Lotus 1-2-3 (a spreadsheet program) uses .WKS, .WK1, and .WK3 for its files. Excel (another spreadsheet program) uses .XLS. Use the DIR command to check the files in each of your program directories to see what extensions are being used.

Program files end in .COM or .EXE. If you were looking for the command to start a program, you could use the **DIR *.EXE** command to list files ending in .EXE. One of these files is probably the one to start the program. To find out more about starting programs, see Chapter 20.

Naming Your Files

Files have a first and a last name. The first name can have up to eight characters (letters, numbers, and other special characters). The last name is used to identify what type of file it is. For example, a word processing file might end in DOC, which is short for document. The last name of a file is called its *extension*, and it can have up to three letters. The first and last names of a file are separated by a period, as in REPORT.DOC.

Use care when naming files, so that you can easily identify them. BUDGET.DOC might not be as descriptive as BUDGET93.DOC, and MEMO.DOC might not be as clear as PRODMEMO.DOC or COPIER.DOC.

What Are Directories?

You organize files on the PC's hard disk just as books are organized in a library. In a library, books are organized by subject. On a computer, files are usually organized by type: *word processing* files are placed in one directory, while *spreadsheet* files are placed in a different directory. In this analogy, a *directory* can be thought of as a shelf where you place your books (files). Typically, you create a directory for each program that you use, although you can organize your files in any way you choose. If you keep related files in the same directory, they are easier to locate and use.

Getting to the Root of Things

There is a special directory that your computer only has one of: the *root directory*. The root directory is the main directory; other directories branch off the root directory. Directories are also called *subdirectories*, because they are subordinate to the one and only root directory.

When you turn on your computer, you are placed in the root directory, so I like to think of the root directory as being the lobby of my computer. From the lobby, I can move to other directories (rooms off the lobby). You can create directories within directories (I think of this as creating a closet in my room).

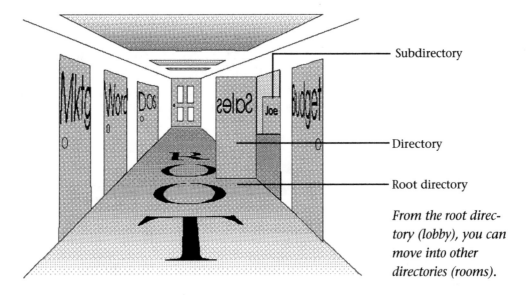

Subdirectory

Directory

Root directory

From the root directory (lobby), you can move into other directories (rooms).

To Get Where You're Going, You Gotta Change Directories

Because each program you own is placed in its own directory, you change directories as you switch from program to program. To change directories, use the CD command (CD stands for change directory). To change directories, type **CD**, then a backslash (\), followed by the name of the directory you want to go to. To change to the DOS directory, use the command

CD\DOS

Root directory   The main or central directory. All other directories branch off the root.

Subdirectories   Means the same thing as directories. The prefix *sub* is used to emphasize the fact that all directories are subordinate to the root directory. Sometimes the word *subdirectories* is used to describe a directory under another directory.

Word processing program   A computer program that is used for typing letters, reports, envelopes, and other tasks that you would normally use a typewriter for.

Spreadsheet program A computer program that organizes information in columns and rows and performs calculations. If you want to balance a checkbook or last year's budget, try using a spreadsheet program.

To change to a directory called WORD, use the command

    CD\WORD

Sometimes, you'll have directories within directories. For example, if your word processing directory is called WORD, you might have a directory within the WORD directory called PROJECTS, to separate the files you create from the rest of the program files (you'll learn to make your own directories in Chapter 12). To change to the PROJECTS directory, you'd have to go through the WORD directory (just as you'd have to go through a bedroom to get to its closet) by using the command

    CD\WORD\PROJECTS

Notice how an additional backslash (\) separates the directory names.

To change to the root directory, type

    CD

The backslash by itself means root directory.

What Goes Wrong When You Change Directories

Basically, only a few things can go wrong when you change directories:

You type a forward slash instead of a backslash.   A backslash looks like this: \ and not /. The backslash is usually located above the Enter key on the right hand side, or on the lower left.

Put It to Work

Using Something Other Than a Greater-Than Sign at the End of Your Prompt

The use of the greater-than sign (>) at the end of a prompt has become something of a standard, but if you don't want it, try one of these substitutions:

If you want to use a less-than sign (<), type **$L.**

If you want to use the pipe (|) or a colon (:), just type | or :. (The pipe character is on the backslash key (\), above the Enter key on most keyboards. If you can't find it there, try looking at the lower left side of your keyboard.)

If you want something really snazzy, like a double arrow (»), try this (but don't press Enter just yet):

PROMPT $P

Now, hold down the **Alt** key and press **175** on the numeric keypad. Release the Alt key, and your command will look like this:

PROMPT $P»

Press **Enter** and you're on your way.

Getting Your Old Prompt Back

If you want to return to a standard DOS prompt (C>), simply reboot the computer (press **Ctrl+Alt+Delete**). If you don't want to reboot, you can type **PROMPT**; and press **Enter**. The semicolon returns you to normal.

If you like your new prompt and want to make it permanent, buy a bag of Snickers (she's getting tired of Ho Ho's) and head for the nearest PC wizard. Have her add the PROMPT command to your AUTOEXEC.BAT file, and it will be set up each time you start your computer. (If you don't add the command to your AUTOEXEC.BAT, you will return to the default system prompt when you reboot.) If you want to save yourself some time (not to mention a fortune in Snickers), why not try editing the AUTOEXEC.BAT yourself? See Chapter 16.

The Least You Need to Know

The jungle of DOS's files and directories will soon become familiar tramping ground if you remember these things:

☞ Files are used to store your work. A file name can contain up to eight characters, followed by a period, and up to a three-character extension, as in BUDGET.DOC.

☞ Directories are places for storing files. You usually create one directory on your hard disk for each program you use.

☞ The root directory is the central, or main, directory.

☞ To change directories, type CD, a backslash (\), and the name of the directory you wish to change to, as in **CD\DOS**.

☞ To change your prompt to display the current drive and directory, use the command **PROMPT PG**.

Chapter 7
Worth the Price of Admission—DOS Shell

In This Chapter

- ☛ Starting and stopping the DOS Shell
- ☛ How to use a mouse with the DOS Shell
- ☛ Changing the DOS Shell display
- ☛ Copying and moving files with the DOS Shell
- ☛ Creating directories with the DOS Shell
- ☛ Deleting files and directories with the DOS Shell
- ☛ Renaming files and directories with the DOS Shell
- ☛ Running programs with the DOS Shell

The DOS Shell is a graphical interface that keeps you safe and warm, miles away from the nasty world of the DOS prompt. Inside the Shell, you can perform the same commands that you could outside the Shell, but with greater ease (and understanding). This chapter is devoted to the DOS Shell, so if you feel you must issue commands at a cold, gray prompt, refer to other chapters to perform these same tasks.

By the Way . . .

Don't let DOS gurus keep you from using the Shell (gurus prefer the prompt because it's what they cut their teeth on). What you'll learn to do with the Shell in this one chapter will take five chapters to learn to do with the DOS prompt, and the Shell's less frustrating!

Once in the Shell, you can get help at any time. Simply press **F1** (that's a function key at the top or left side of your keyboard). Press **Esc** to exit a help screen.

A Word to DOS 4 Users

If you have DOS 4, make things easy on yourself and upgrade to DOS 6. DOS 6 includes many nifty features for the first-time user, and the DOS 6 Shell (featured in this chapter) is much easier to use than the DOS 4 Shell. (Some of the things you'll learn in this chapter are different for DOS 4 Shell users.) If you're interested in DOS 6, see Chapter 8 for more details.

Playing the Shell Game

You can start the DOS Shell by typing (yes, you guessed it)

> **DOSSHELL**

If you get the error message **Bad command or file name**, DOS can't find the Shell program. Type the command

> **CD\DOS**

and press **Enter**. Then type

> **DOSSHELL**

> To have the DOS Shell run automatically at startup (so you won't even have to see that nasty ol' DOS prompt), add the DOSSHELL command to your AUTOEXEC.BAT. Don't know how? Have someone show you, or refer to Chapter 16.

To learn how to set up a DOS path so things like this won't happen again, refer to Chapter 4.

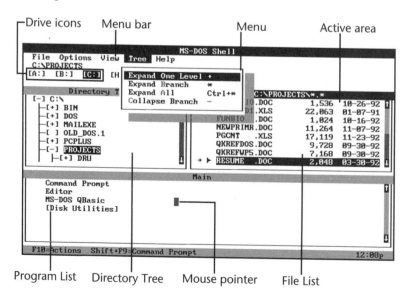

The DOS 6 Shell in all its beauty.

Making Friends with a Mouse

Using the Shell without a mouse is like trying to pull something out of the oven without oven mitts. It can be done, but why take the chance of getting burned? So if you plan on using the Shell, get a *mouse!*

To use the mouse, you either *click* or *double-click* with the left mouse button. Some actions require that you *drag* the mouse (no, not along the floor—along the mouse pad!).

Would You Like to See a Menu?

One of the best things about the DOS Shell is that you don't type commands; instead, you just select something off a menu, and it's done! Look back at the picture of the DOS Shell screen. You'll find a menu bar hanging around the top of the screen with five choices: File, Options, View, Tree, and Help. I've opened the Tree menu for you, and selected the command of the day, Expand One Level.

Mouse   A device attached to your computer that controls a pointer on your screen. To move the pointer to the left, move the mouse to the left. To move the pointer to the right, move the mouse to the right, and so on.

Click   To click with the mouse, press the mouse button once.

Double-click   To double-click with the mouse, press the mouse button twice in rapid succession.

Drag   To drag with the mouse, first move the mouse pointer to the starting position. Now click and hold the mouse button. Drag the mouse pointer to the ending position, and then release the mouse button.

Open All Night: Shell Menus

You don't even have to know what you want to do in the Shell; you can just open a menu and browse. To open a menu, click on the menu name with your mouse.

Once the menu is open, you can select whatever you want (go ahead, I'm buyin'). To select a command, click on the command name with your mouse.

Put It to Work
Everyone Has a Right to Change Modes

Here's an exercise that'll help you practice using menus and —better yet—you get to play around with the video! When you start the DOS Shell, it starts in *text mode* (a display mode that uses lines and such to show screen elements). If your PC has a monitor that supports graphics, you can change the DOS Shell display to *graphics mode* (a display mode that uses pictures and boxes to show screen elements). Warning: Graphics mode may not be suitable for younger viewers.

You can also select from several screen *resolutions*, which determine the number of text lines that fit on your screen at once. The higher the resolution you select, the smaller (and harder to read!) the text on your screen will appear.

To change the DOS Shell to a different video mode, follow these steps:

1. Open the **O**ptions menu. (Click on it, or press **Alt+O**.)

2. Select the **D**isplay command. (Click on it, or press **D**.)

3. Choose the mode you want. Either click on it, or use the arrow keys to highlight it.

4. Click on **OK** or press **Enter**. The screen changes to the resolution you selected.

This Screen Display Mode box lets you select a video mode.

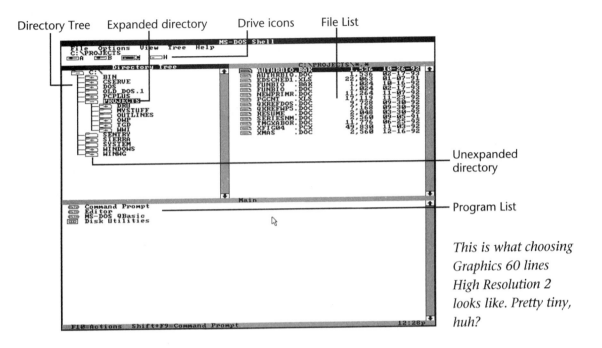

Directory Tree   Expanded directory   Drive icons   File List

Unexpanded directory

Program List

This is what choosing Graphics 60 lines High Resolution 2 looks like. Pretty tiny, huh?

Moving Between the Areas on the Screen

Now that you've mastered menus, let's look at the rest of the screen. As I take you through our guided tour, imagine that the Shell is a house with many rooms. Unfortunately, it's a house furnished by DOS, so it doesn't come with electricity. DOS isn't totally cruel; we've got one flashlight, and we can shine it on any room we want to use. To work in an area of the Shell (a room), you must move the cursor (the flashlight) to that area. Moving the cursor to an area *activates* the area (lights it up).

The Shell screen is divided into several areas:

The Drive icons area, where you choose which drive to show.

The Directory Tree, which shows the directories on the chosen drive.

The Tree menu is used to expand and contract subdirectories. For example, in the picture above, the PROJECTS directory is expanded, showing the subdirectory DRU. A minus indicates a directory that is displaying its subdirectories, and a plus indicates a directory that is hiding them. Use the plus and the minus keys to expand and contract a directory.

The File List, which shows the files in the chosen directory.

The Program List, which lists programs set up to run from the DOS Shell.

The active area shows up highlighted on-screen. Looking back at the first picture in the chapter, you can see that the File List area is active, because its title bar (the part that says C:\PROJECTS *.*) is darker than the title bars of the other areas.

To move from room to room in your house of shells, just click anywhere within that area with the mouse.

Displaying Files on a Different Drive

Now that we've got the run of the house, let's see what we can see. The disk drive that you're currently looking at is highlighted at the top of the screen. To display files on a different drive, click on that drive in the Drive Icons area.

Displaying Files in a Different Directory

Selecting the right drive may get you into the neighborhood, but the Directory Tree will get you to the right house. The directory you select in the Directory Tree determines which files will show up in the File List area.

To choose a different directory from the Directory Tree area, just click on a directory with your mouse.

If you see a plus sign in front of a directory, that means that there are some subdirectories hiding. You can make them show their faces by clicking on the plus sign with your mouse.

Selecting Files to Work On

Before you can do something to a file (for instance, copy it or delete it), you need to select it. You can select one file or lots of files; whatever you want to work on. To select a single file, just give that file a little click. To select several files, hold down the **Ctrl** key while you click on the files, one by one, with your mouse. Then release the Ctrl key.

Copying Files

When you copy files, the original file is left where it is, and a copy is placed where you indicate. For example, you might want to copy files to a different directory or disk as a backup.

Don't forget to hold down the **Ctrl** key when copying files with the mouse, or you may end up moving them instead!

To copy files with the mouse, select them, and then hold down the **Ctrl** key. Drag the copies where you want them. (You can drag them to a drive icon in the Drive Icons area or to a directory on the Directory Tree.) When the confirmation box appears, click on the **Yes** button.

Moving Files

When you move files, the files are relocated where you indicate. For example, you might want to move files that you seldom use into a different directory to get them out of your way.

To move files with the mouse, select them, hold the **Alt** key down, then drag the files to their new home. You can drag them to either a different drive in the Drive Icons area or a directory on the Directory Tree. When the confirmation box appears, click on the **Yes** button.

Creating New Directories

In Chapter 6, you learned all about directories and how you use them to organize your files. You can create a directory under the root directory (a room right off the lobby) or a subdirectory under an existing directory (a closet within an existing room). With the Shell, it's easy to remodel! Just follow me:

1. Click on the Directory Tree area, and highlight the root directory (or the existing directory that the new directory should appear under).

2. Click on the File menu to open it.

3. Click on the Create Directory command.

4. Type the name of the new directory (up to eight characters), and click **OK**.

Deleting Files and Directories

When a file or a directory is no longer useful, get rid of it. Directories are always the last ones to leave a party. To get a directory to go, you must delete the files in the directory first.

To delete files, select them and press the **Delete** or **Del** key. If you selected more than one file, click on **OK** or press **Enter**. To confirm the deletion of each file, click on the **Yes** button; to skip a file, click on the **No** button.

A file name can contain up to eight characters, followed by a period, and up to a three-character extension (for example, APRBUDGT.WKS). A directory name follows the same rules, but most people do not give a directory name an extension. For example, GAMES or PROJECTS are common directory names.

After all the files are gone and the directory is empty, highlight it on the Directory Tree and press **Del**. Click the **Yes** button when you're asked for confirmation.

Renaming Files or Directories

If you don't like the name of a file or a directory, change it!

First, select the file or directory. Then open the File menu and select the Re**name** command by clicking on them. Type the new name in the box that appears, and then press **Enter**.

Running Programs

You can select a program to run using several methods, but the easiest way is to use the Program List (located at the bottom of the screen). Within the Program List, double-click on the program's name to start the program.

If you want to run a program that's not listed on the Program List and don't have time to wait for someone to set it up for you, here's an alternate method:

☞ Double-click on the program file in the File List (for example, click on **WORD.EXE** to run Microsoft Word).

Exiting the DOS Shell

To exit the DOS Shell and return to the cold, gray world of the DOS prompt (C>), press **F3**. (That's a function key at the top or left side of your keyboard.)

If you have a mouse (and you really should), open the File menu and select the Exit command.

The easiest way to run programs is through the Program List, but it's a little tricky to set up. Bug someone to help you customize it with the programs you want to run.

TECHNO NERD TEACHES

DOS 5 and 6 come with neat task swappers that allow you to run more than one program at a time and to switch between them. For example, you could start a letter in your word processing program, switch to your spreadsheet program to calculate some numbers, then return to your letter. Task swapping is beyond what you need to know (it's even beyond the scope of this book). If you can talk someone into setting up your Program List, have them show you how to use the task swapper.

The Least You Need to Know

You'll be picking up sea shells by the DOS Shell shore when you remember these tips:

- ☞ Start the DOS Shell by typing **DOSSHELL**.

- ☞ Change directories by clicking on them.

- ☞ Select multiple files by holding the **Ctrl** key while you click on them.

- ☞ Holding down the **Alt** key while dragging files moves them; holding down the **Ctrl** key while dragging files copies them.

- ☞ Create directories with the **File Create Directory** command; delete them with the **Del** key.

- ☞ Rename files and directories with the **File Rename** command.

- ☞ Run programs by selecting them from the Program List, usually located at the bottom of the Shell screen.

- ☞ Exit the DOS Shell with the **File Exit** command.

Chapter 8
That's My Version and I'm Stickin' to It

In This Chapter

- ☛ How to determine the DOS version your PC uses
- ☛ Highlights from the latest DOS version—DOS 6
- ☛ How to access DOS help

In this chapter, you'll learn about DOS versions—what the differences are and how to tell which one you have. After making you read a shameless plug for upgrading to DOS 6, I'll tell you how to access DOS's built-in Help system (versions 5 and above only).

What's a Version?

Every year or so, software manufacturers update their products. To distinguish one year's model from another, they assign version numbers. DOS is no exception—new versions come rolling out of Microsoft every few years.

The most recently released version is MS-DOS 6. You'll learn about it later in this chapter.

TECHNO NERD TEACHES

MS-DOS version 1.0 was the first, back in 1980. Since then, there have been eight major releases: DOS 2.0, DOS 3.0, 3.1, 3.2, and 3.3, DOS 4.01, DOS 5.0, and DOS 6.0. Each version improved on its ancestors by adding more features and supporting more kinds of hardware. For example, the earliest versions of DOS didn't support hard disks (they weren't invented yet), and up until version 4.0, DOS did not support large hard disks (bigger than 30 megabytes).

What Version Are You?

If you followed the example in Chapter 2, you've already learned what version of DOS you have. If not, type this command and press **Enter**:

VER

You should see something like this:

MS-DOS Version 6.00

(or whatever version you have, if not 6.00).

The DOS 25th Anniversary Show: A Blast from DOS's Past

Okay, I admit I'm about 12 years early for a 25th anniversary show, but I thought you might like to know something about the DOS version you own (if you're not lucky enough to own DOS 6).

Hey, I told you this chapter would be a shameless plug for DOS 6, and it will, but what better selling tool than to point out the pathetic lack of features in earlier versions? Really, unless you have an *"aversion"* to it, I'd save myself a lot of cares and woes and upgrade to DOS 6. Okay, enough. Any more of this, and Microsoft will have to put me on their payroll.

DOS on parade.

DOS Version	Nominations for best new DOS feature	What the critics say
1.0	Single-sided diskette drives	Golly, Gomer, welcome to the computer age.
1.1	Double-sided diskette drives	You mean I can use both sides without flipping it? Talk about convenience!
2.0	Hard disk support	A diskette that stays in the computer? It's just a fad—it'll never catch on.

DOS Version	Nominations for best new DOS feature	What the critics say
3.0	High-density 5 1/4-inch diskettes	What am I gonna do with all this room?
3.3	3 1/2-inch diskettes	So I can still use my 5 1/4-inch disks if I fold them, right?
4.0	Support for hard drives over 32MB	You've got to be kidding! Heck, we'll never need more than 32MB!
5.0	Upper and expanded memory support	You mean I can use conventional memory to *run programs* and not DOS? Gosh! All this, and a Shell, a help system, and a full-screen editor. I'll never ask for more (until DOS 6).

The Best and the Brightest: DOS 6

DOS 6 is the latest version of DOS. Here's a list of some of its features:

Improved help system   The new help system provides descriptions, syntax, and examples of each DOS command. You don't even have to look in the manual! You'll learn how to use the DOS help system later in this chapter.

Improved capability to undelete files   With DOS 6, you stand a better chance of being able to recover files that you have deleted accidentally. How does this magic work? Refer to Chapter 11 for more information.

Backing up   A process that copies your files onto diskettes in a special compressed format. If something bad happens to the originals, you can restore your backed-up files (a process that uncompresses the files and copies them back).

Restoring   Backing up your files is a process that copies files onto diskettes in a special compressed format. If those files become damaged somehow, you can restore them through a reverse process that uncompresses the backed-up files and copies them back.

System backup and restore   Since computer data is stored electronically, there's no sense in taking chances. DOS 6 comes with an easy-to-use *backup* program with a graphical interface that makes backing up your system a breeze. You'll learn more about backing up and *restoring* in Chapters 14 and 15.

Virus protection   A *virus* is a computer program whose sole purpose is to wreak havoc on your computer system. A computer virus is no laughing matter, and protecting your system against a virus is an important job. DOS 6 comes with built-in virus protection. You'll learn more about virus protection in Chapter 17.

Improved memory management   *Memory* (RAM) is the working area of your PC. RAM is your computer's desktop; every program and every file must be placed on the desktop (loaded into memory) before the computer can use it. Effective management of this precious resource improves the speed and efficiency that your computer processes information with. DOS 6 comes with a built-in memory manager that makes customizing memory for your specific needs a breeze. You'll learn more about memory management in Chapter 19.

Disk compression   Files can be compressed (shrunk) so that they take up less room on your hard drive. With disk compression, you can almost double the amount of data you can store on your hard disk. DOS 6 comes with a disk compression program.

By the Way . . .

Okay, if you just gotta have it, a DOS 6 upgrade package is available at the nearest software dealer, probably for less than a hundred bucks.

Help, I Need Somebody!

If you have at least DOS version 5, you can access DOS help. Type the command you want help on, followed by the switch /?. For example, if you need help with the DIR command, type

DIR /?

You'll see a listing of possible switches and parameters that can be used with the command. You can also type

HELP DIR

With DOS 5, if you type **HELP** followed by a command name, you get the same result as if you used the /? switch. But with DOS 6, you get the new, improved (now with 50% less fat) DOS 6 help system.

Using the DOS 6 Help System

When you first access the DOS 6 help system, you see a listing of the syntax and the parameters for a command. Press **Page Down** to see more (press **Page Up** to go back).

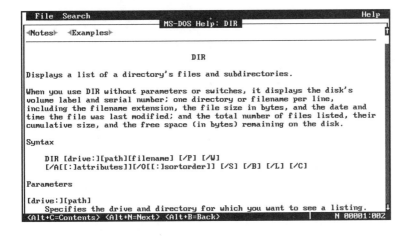

The new, improved DOS 6 help system.

SPEAK LIKE A GEEK

Jump term A highlighted term in the DOS 6 help system that, when selected, "jumps" to a related section of the help system.

If you see a word in angle brackets, such as <Tree>, it is a *jump term*. Press **Tab** until the cursor moves to a jump term, then press **Enter** to select it. You will move to another section of the help system that contains information about the jump term.

On the first page of every command, you will see **Notes** and **Examples**. Notes lists additional tips and cautions about using the command. Examples lists several ways to type the command. Use the **Tab** key until the cursor moves to either of these items, and press **Enter** to select it.

To exit the help system and return to a DOS prompt, press the **Alt** key, and then press the letter **F**. The File menu will be displayed. Press **X** to select Exit. (This works just like it did in the DOS Shell in Chapter 7!)

The Least You Need to Know

Glad you could join me! Would you care for a nightcap— I mean a recap? You learned:

- ☛ To tell what DOS version your system is using, use the **VER** command.

- ☛ DOS 6 includes many enhancements that make it easier to use your PC, especially if you are a first-time user: an improved help system and an easy-to-use backup system for protecting your files.

- ☛ DOS 6 also provides some thoughtful enhancements, such as a virus-protection program, a program that customizes your system's memory usage, and a disk compression program that saves disk space.

- ☛ Both DOS 5 and DOS 6 include help for each command. Type the command name followed by /? to get help. For example, type **DIR /?**.

- ☛ DOS 6 includes a more extensive help system than DOS 5, which is accessed by typing **HELP** followed by the command. For example, type **HELP DIR**.

Part Two
A Daily Dose of DOS

In this section, you'll find everything you need to know about completing daily tasks with DOS. Since one-third of the job of using a computer is maintaining and organizing your information (PCs should come with a maid), this section of the book will be your most used. Each chapter is chock-full of exactly what you need to know to maintain your files, your directories, and your sanity.

Although you'll use this section a lot, you probably won't remember how to use every command. (The only thing that's EASY about DOS is forgetting everything you did the last time you used a particular command.) So read and then forget; everything you need to know will still be there when you need it again.

Chapter 9

Lost Something?
How to Find Files with
the DIR Command

In This Chapter

- Listing files one screenful at a time
- Understanding the DIR file listing
- Listing files on another drive or directory
- Listing files across the screen
- Listing files in alphabetical order
- Looking for selected files in a directory
- Printing a file listing

This chapter is all about listing and finding files with the DOS command DIR. Using the DIR command is like reading a table of contents for a book—it's a great way to become familiar with your PC and find out what's on it.

Also, if you've ever had the frustrating experience of misplacing a file that you were working on just moments ago, those times are past. This chapter will show you how to find lost files and lots more stuff. Learn how to print a list of all the files in a directory or on a diskette. Look inside a file to see what's in it, to find out if it's a file you need, or just to satisfy an itchy curiosity.

Some Things You Should Know About the DIR Command

So you don't have to go scrambling back to previous chapters, here's a quick review of some important concepts:

Remember to press Enter to execute a command.   Until you press Enter, nothing will happen.

The DIR command is made up of three parts: The command itself (DIR), parameters (specific file names you want listed), and switches (a forward slash (/) followed by a letter; switches modify the DIR command to make it display files in several ways). Separate each part with a space.

The DIR command lists files in the current directory or drive unless you specify otherwise.   If you don't specify a different directory or drive, DOS assumes the DIR command refers to the current drive and directory. To switch drives so you can list files on another drive, type the drive letter followed by a colon, as in

> **A:**

To switch directories, type **CD** followed by the name of the directory that you want to go to, as in

> **CD\\DOS**

OR

> **CD\\WORD\\PROJECTS**

Why and When You'd Want to Use the DIR Command

I thought I'd interrupt this potentially boring stuff to remind you why you might want to use the DIR command in the first place. Here are some reasons:

DIR is an easy way to see an overview of what's on your hard disk.   Use the DIR command to list all of the main directories on a disk.

Because there is usually a directory for each program, this list helps you figure out what *programs* you have available (see "Locating a Lost Directory").

DIR helps you figure out how to start a new program.   Use the DIR command to find the file that starts the program (see "Listing Selected Files").

You can locate files with DIR.   Files get lost. How? How can a memo get lost in an In-basket? Who knows? It just does. So sometime, someday, you'll want the fastest way to find a misplaced file, and that's the DIR command (see "Locating a File Across Several Directories").

DIR helps you identify diskettes.   If you forget to label your diskettes (like I do), the only way to tell what they contain is by using the DIR command (see "Listing Files on Another Drive").

Which is the latest copy? DIR knows.   If you have several copies of the same file, the DIR command can tell you which copy is the most current (just check out the date).

DIR is easy to use.   Only three letters: D-I-R. Gotta love a command like that!

Listing All the Files in a Directory

Listing all of the files within the current directory is the computer equivalent of reading a soup label. How else are you going to find what's on the disk? Simply type

DIR /P

By the Way . . .

Other books will tell you to simply type **DIR** and be done with it, but you'll usually end up with files scrolling off your screen if you do. That's why I automatically add the /**P** switch, which means, "List all the files until they fill the screen, then pause."

If this directory has a lot of files to list, you'll see the message **Press any key to continue . . .** Press **Enter** when you are ready to see the rest of the files in the directory.

What Does It All Mean? (Understanding the DIR Listing)

Using the DIR command is easy. Understanding what it's trying to tell you is not. Here's what a DOS directory listing typically looks like and what it contains:

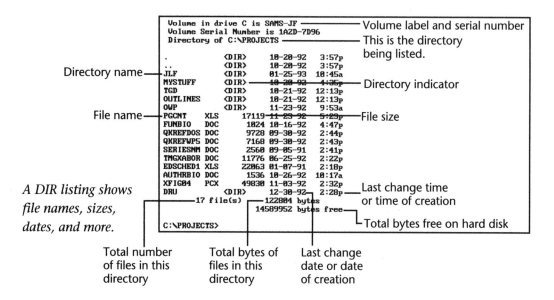

A DIR listing shows file names, sizes, dates, and more.

Volume in drive C is SAMS-JF   The *volume label* is the name that was given to the disk when it was *formatted* (prepared for use). Your PC may be called something equally as clever, or nothing at all (names are not required). This is followed by the volume's serial number (a number that is generated when the disk is formatted).

Directory of C:\PROJECTS   This line is very important; it tells you what drive and directory are being listed.

File or directory name   The first column lists file and directory names. File names consist of a first and last name, separated by a period, as in PGCNT.XLS. However, in the DIR listing, this same file is displayed as

PGCNT   XLS

with several spaces separating the first and last names, instead of the usual period.

<DIR> indicator   The <DIR> notation marks subdirectories (directories that are under this directory).

File size   This column lists each file's size in *bytes*. A total of all the files in this directory is displayed at the bottom of the listing. Subdirectories do not have a file size; their size is determined by the files within them.

> ## By the Way . . .
> I used to forget what a byte, kilobyte, and megabyte are, so I thought you might like a reminder. A byte is equal to a single character, like 4, J, or %. A kilobyte is about 1,000 bytes (it's really 1,024 bytes for you sticklers out there). A megabyte is about 1,000,000 bytes. (Okay, it's really 1,048,576 bytes.)

Last change date   This date tells you when a subdirectory was created or when a file was created or last changed.

Last change time   This is like the last change date, telling you what time a subdirectory was created or what time a file was last changed.

Total files   At the end of the DIR listing, you'll see the total number of files in the directory, along with the total number of bytes being used by the files. Subdirectories are counted as files, too, so if a directory has two subdirectories and three files, you'll see a total of five files. However, DOS likes to keep things interesting, so although subdirectories are counted for total files, their contents are not counted in total bytes.

Total bytes free   This one's self-explanatory; it's the number of bytes of free space left on the disk.

Listing Files on Another Drive

When you're "talking" to DOS through the command prompt, it assumes that the current drive and directory is the "subject" of your conversation. That's why you get a listing of the files in the root directory of your hard disk when you type **DIR** at the **C:\>** prompt.

A quicker way to list files on another drive is to include the drive letter to list with the DIR command. So instead of changing to drive A, simply type

DIR A:

Because you specified drive A, the files on drive A will be listed instead of those on C. This saves you the trouble of switching between drives.

To list files on another drive, you can change to that drive by typing the drive letter followed by a colon (:). For example, if you were in drive C but you wanted to list the files on a diskette in drive A, you would type

   A:

and press **Enter**. The prompt changes to **A:\>** or to some variation of that. Then you could use the DIR command to list the files in drive A, because the drive A is now the current drive.

  When you are ready to switch back to your original drive, type the drive letter followed by a colon (:), as in

   C:

And your prompt would return to **C:\>** (or something similar).

Listing Files in Another Directory

By default, DIR lists files in the current directory only. To see the contents of a different directory, either you must make the desired directory active by changing to that directory, or you must specify its name with the DIR command.

First, let's try it by changing to the desired directory, using the CD command. For example, to change to the 123 directory, type

CD \123

and press **Enter**. This command changes you to the 123 directory. To get the directory listing, type

DIR /P

This command lists the files for the current directory. To get back to your original directory, you would have to use the CD command to change directories again.

You can get dizzy changing directories all the time, so an easier way is to include the directory name with the DIR command. For example, if you wanted to list the files in the 123 directory without leaving the directory you're in, you would type

DIR \123 /P

Even though you might be in, say, the WORD directory, the files in the 123 directory would be listed instead. It's like seeing into the next room without actually going into that room. This command comes in handy for lousy typists like me (I don't want to type any more than necessary).

Listing Files Across the Screen

Sometimes, you don't need all the information that the DIR command provides. If you are looking for a file, it is simpler to look at only the file names. Try this command:

DIR /W /P

The /W switch modifies the DIR command so file names display across the screen in wide format. The /P switch is optional, but I use it just in case there's more than one screenful of names. After I use this command, my screen looks like this:

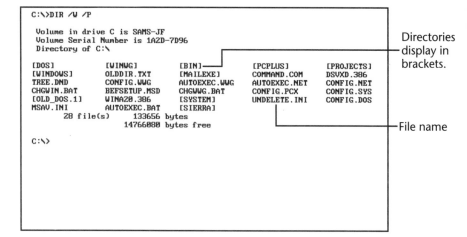

Displaying file names in a wide format shows fewer details, but more files can fit on-screen at the same time.

Listing Files in Alphabetical Order

Files normally display in the order in which they are stored on disk, which is about as useful as a calendar without months. *If you have at least DOS version 5,* you can force DOS to display the files in some kind of reasonable order, such as, dare we say it, *alphabetically*. Use this command:

DIR /O /P

This command lists subdirectories first, then files, sorted by first name.

Put It to Work

Customizing the DIR Command

This project is for people with DOS 5 or above. Because you now know that you'll use the DIR command often, you can customize the DIR command to the way you work. I always add the /P switch to the DIR command to prevent the file listing from scrolling off the screen. You can customize the DIR command so that the /P switch is added automatically without you having to type it each time.

Type this command at the DOS prompt:

SET DIRCMD=/P

From then on, all you have to type is

DIR

and you'll really get DIR /P.

To return to plain old DIR with no customizing, type

SET DIRCMD=

If you like it, keep it by adding this command to your AUTOEXEC.BAT file. Do-it-yourselfers should read Chapter 16 for details.

Listing Selected Files

If you're looking for a particular file, or a particular file type (extension), you can use *wild cards* to list selected files.

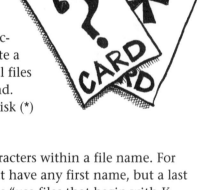

A *wild card* is used to represent characters within a file name. Wild cards create a general file name pattern so that several files can be used with a single DOS command. There are two DOS wild cards: the asterisk (*) and the question mark (?).

The asterisk * represents several characters within a file name. For example, *.DOC means "use files that have any first name, but a last name of DOC." Using K*.DOC means "use files that begin with K, followed by a bunch of miscellaneous characters that have a last name of DOC. Using *.* means "use files with any first or last name," in other words, "use all the files." Any characters after an asterisk are ignored, so M*RCH.* is the same as M*.*.

The question mark ? is used to represent a single character within a file name. For example, JO?N.WKS means "use files that begin with the letters JO, followed by any character, followed by an N, and the extension .WKS." The files JOHN.WKS and JOAN.WKS match this pattern, but the files JEAN.WKS and JOHNNY.WKS do not. You can use additional question marks to represent other characters, as in JO??.WKS, but the number of characters must also match. The files JOHN.WKS, JOKE.WKS and JOAN.WKS would match this file name pattern, but JOKES.WKS would not.

To list selected files, simply type **DIR** followed by the file name pattern, as in

DIR TAXES??.* /P

This command lists (one screenful at a time) all the files in the current directory that start with the letters TAXES, followed by two characters, and any extension.

Put It to Work

Starting a New Program When You're Not Sure What Command to Type

If you've found a new program on your hard drive but no one is around to tell you how to start it, change to that directory and try this command:

DIR * .EXE /P

This will list the program files; look for one that matches the name of the directory (or comes close), such as WP.EXE, 123.EXE, and so on. Type its name, as in

WP

and the program will probably start. If you don't find an .EXE file, look for a file that ends in .BAT or .COM.

Locating a File Across Several Directories

My mom created a letter one day, saved it, and went to lunch. When she came back, the letter file was gone! She figured that maybe she hadn't saved it properly, so she retyped it, saved it again, and took a coffee break.

When she returned, the letter file was nowhere to be found. Just as she was ready to look for the prankster who was messing with her files, a friend came over and showed her the following command. Her files were there; they were simply in the wrong directory!

If you have at least DOS version 5, you can use this command to locate a file anywhere on your hard disk. For example, to find the file LOST.DOC, you would type

DIR C:\LOST.DOC /S /P

The /S switch tells DIR to look in the current directory, and all subdirectories. By adding C:\ in front of the file name, DIR will not start in the current directory, but in the root directory (neat, eh?).

By the Way . . .

You could probably leave the /P switch off this time (unless there are so many copies of LOST.DOC all over your hard drive, that you expect the listing to scroll off the screen).

You can use wild cards to conduct more extensive searches. For example, if you want to list all the .DOC files on your hard disk, type

DIR C:*.DOC /S /P

Locating a Lost Directory

Directories (especially subdirectories) can get lost, too. Because most hard disks today are so large, directories have a lot of space to hide in. Use this command to find the directory LOSTDIR (you must have at least DOS 5.0 to use this command):

DIR C:\LOSTDIR. /S /P

This command translates to "List all the files that begin LOSTDIR and have no extension, beginning with the root directory, going across all directories, one screenful at a time." Because directories don't usually have extensions (last names), look for a "file" with no extension, and you'll probably get a directory. To list all the directories on a hard disk, use this command:

DIR C:*. /S /P

If you have at least DOS 5, you can print a file listing with the name of each file appearing on a separate line, going down—instead of across—the paper. Use this command:

DIR A: /B > PRN

Printing a File Listing

When you use the DIR command (or any other command, for that matter), the result of that command is displayed on the monitor. You can redirect the output to a different device, such as your printer. Why do this? Sometimes it's easier to flip pages than to scan through a directory listing on-screen. Also, a printout of their contents makes a great way to organize diskettes. To send a listing of all the files on a diskette to the printer, use this command:

DIR A: /W >PRN

The greater-than sign (>) is the *redirection symbol*; PRN is DOS's name for your printer. Because you'll probably want to print only the file names (and not the other DIR information), I included the /W switch.

You can also send the file listing to another file, so you can save it permanently, or print it out later. To save a listing of the current directory in a file, use a command like this:

DIR >FILE.LST

The Least You Need to Know

I gotta admit, the DIR command is one of my favorites (probably 'cause it's so easy to spell). But seriously, look at all the stuff you learned about the DIR command:

☞ To list the files in a directory, type **DIR /P**.

☞ The DIR command lists the files in the current directory only. To list files on another drive, use a command like this: **DIR A: /P**. To list files in another directory, use a command like this: **DIR \PROJECTS /P**.

☞ The file listing includes the name of the file or directory; followed by its size; and then the date and time that file or directory was created or the file was changed. The file listing also displays the total number of files in the directory and the amount of space left on the disk.

☞ To list file names across the screen, type **DIR /W /P**.

☞ If you have at least DOS 5, use this command to list files alphabetically: **DIR /O /P**.

☞ If you have at least DOS 5, you can customize your DIR command by including something like this in your AUTOEXEC.BAT: **SET DIRCMD=/P**.

☞ The DOS wild cards, * and ?, can be used with the DIR command. The * replaces several characters in a file name, and ? replaces only one. For example, DIR JOE?.* lists files like JOE1.DOC, JOE2.DOC, and JOES.WKS.

☞ You can locate a file anywhere on your hard disk by typing something like this: **DIR C:\LOST.DOC /S /P**.

☞ Create a paper listing of your files by adding **>PRN** to the end of the **DIR** command.

Chapter 10

Standing at the Copier, Copying Files

In This Chapter

- Making a duplicate of a file
- Copying files from one directory to another
- Copying files to a diskette
- Copying files to a directory
- Copying files from one diskette to another
- Renaming files
- Moving files

This chapter is all about copying files, one of the most common DOS tasks. Copy files onto a diskette for safekeeping or copy files from a diskette to your hard disk so you can access them more quickly. When you copy a file, the original file stays where it is, and a copy is placed in the location you indicate. If you want to move a file instead of copy it, the last section in this chapter gives you easy instructions on how to move files.

By the Way . . .

I once had a friend who was having trouble with one of her document files. I asked her to make a copy and send it to me so I could take a look at it. When I opened the interoffice mail the next day, I found a photocopy of the diskette! (I guess I should have been more specific.)

continues

continued

Because the COPY command is one of the hardest DOS commands to get right, I've included many examples. Just follow the examples and substitute the names of your directories and files (and hopefully, you'll find the process pretty painless).

Things You Should Know About the COPY Command

So you don't have to go scrambling back to previous chapters, here's a quick review of some important concepts:

Remember to press Enter to execute a command.   Until you press Enter, nothing will happen.

The COPY command is made up of three parts: The command itself (COPY), followed by the name of the file(s) to copy, followed by the place to copy the file(s) to.

The COPY command overwrites existing files without telling you.   Be careful or you'll overwrite existing files with the same names.

Naming your copy.   When you copy a file, you are making a duplicate of the original. You can give the duplicate a new name, or let it keep its original name (*but no two files can have the same name, unless they are in different directories or on different disks*).

The COPY command copies files FROM/TO the current directory or drive, unless you specify otherwise.   You can include other directories and drives (*path names*) as part of the file name, though, as you'll see in this chapter.

The most common error message you get when using the COPY command is File not found.   If you get this error message, try using the full path name for the file; maybe the file is not in this directory. If needed, use the DIR command to list the files in the current directory so you can check the spelling; maybe you misspelled the name of the file.

Path Finders: One Way for DOS to Locate a File

Using a path to designate a file is like telling a friend how to find your house. A path name consists of three parts:

The drive the file is located on followed by a colon, as in C:.

A backslash (\) followed by the complete path to the file. Start with the parent directory, then add another backslash, and a subdirectory name if applicable. Finish up with a final backslash, as in **\PROJECTS\DOSBOOK**.

End the path name with a file name or file specification, as in **CHAPTR08.DOC**.

The completed path would look like this:

C:\PROJECTS\DOSBOOK\CHAPTR08.DOC

The COPY Command—Gotta Love It!

Before you wade through all this stuff about copying files, I thought you might like to know why you'd want to use the COPY command in the first place. Here's a list of what comes to mind:

COPY can create duplicates of important files before they get ruined.   Files like your AUTOEXEC.BAT and CONFIG.SYS (which you paid several Ho Ho's to obtain) are important and hard to reconstruct from scratch. Safeguard them against disasters by copying them (see "Cloning 101: Making a Duplicate of a File"). Better yet, copy them onto a diskette (see "Copying Files from a Directory to a Diskette").

COPY makes room for a new program.   If you have more than one disk drive, such as C or D, you may want to move files from one drive to another. The COPY command can help you (see "Copying a File from One Directory to Another"). If you're simply out of room, you can copy files onto diskettes and then delete them from your hard disk (see "Copying Files from a Directory to a Diskette").

With COPY, you can keep your versions straight.   Before you make changes to an important document, you might want to put the original in a separate directory, in case you want to refer to it later. Use the COPY command to copy a backup into a separate directory. Then you can make changes with confidence (see "Copying a File from One Directory to Another").

With COPY, you can use your files on a different PC.   If your PC doesn't have the program or printer to finish the job, use the COPY command to copy the file onto a diskette, so you can transfer the file to another PC. The COPY command is also great for sharing documents with co-workers (see "Copying Files from a Directory to a Diskette").

Cloning 101: Making a Duplicate of a File

The simplest form of the COPY command is used to make a copy of a file, placed in the same directory but with a different name. For example, to make a backup copy of your AUTOEXEC.BAT file, you could type this:

COPY AUTOEXEC.BAT AUTOEXEC.BKP

File not found? You may be in the wrong directory. The COPY command assumes that you are in the directory where the file to copy is located. If you're not, you need to include the complete path to the file name, as in

COPY C:\AUTOEXEC.BAT C:\AUTOEXEC.BKP

If the COPY command is successful, you'll see the message **1 file(s) copied**. If not, you may get **File not found**.

The two parameters of the COPY command act like the "From" side and the "To" side of a gift tag. This command translates as "Copy the file AUTOEXEC.BAT *from* the current directory, *to* the current directory, and call the copy AUTOEXEC.BKP." Because you didn't type any explicit directory locations, COPY assumes you mean a "From" file and a "To" file in the current directory.

Cloning an Army: Duplicating Several Files at Once

You can use DOS *wild cards* to specify more than one file to copy. Wild cards create a general file name pattern so that several files can be used with a single DOS command. There are two DOS wild cards, the asterisk (*) and the question mark (?). The asterisk * represents several characters within a file name (as in *.WKS), and the question mark ? represents a single character within a file name (as in CHAP??.DOC).

For example, suppose you want to create a duplicate of all the .WK1 files in the \SPREADST directory. Follow these steps:

CD\SPREADST
COPY *.WK1 *.BKP

This command creates a copy of all the files in the current directory with an extension of .WK1, and changes the extension on the copy to .BKP. Use wild cards in place of file names in any COPY command to copy multiple files at once.

> ### By the Way . . .
>
> If you want to copy the files in one step, without changing the directory, include the full path names:
>
> **COPY C:\SPREADSHT*.WK1 C:\SPREADSHT*.BK1**
>
> Whew! Even though you save a step, it's a lot more typing. Choose whichever is easier for you.

From Here to Eternity: Variations on a Copy

The basic parts of the COPY command never change:

COPY[space]*what you're copying*[space]*where to place the copy*

Here are some basic rules to keep in mind:

- ☛ If you don't specify a drive (for both the "what" and the "where to" parts), DOS assumes you mean the current drive.

- ☛ If you don't specify a directory, DOS assumes you mean the current directory.

- ☛ You have to specify a file name (or file name pattern, if you want to copy several files) for the "what to copy" part. If you want to make the name of the copy different from the original's, specify a new name in the "where to copy" part.

Ready for some examples? Here we go.

Copying a File from One Directory to Another

Suppose you want to work on an important document and to protect your originals, you always copy them into a directory called (cleverly enough) ORIG. After copying the original to a safe place, you can work on the copy without fear of losing anything to the great DOS abyss. You need to copy the file BIGBUDGT.WK1 from the \SPREADST directory to a directory called \SPREADST\ORIG. Follow these steps:

First, go to the source directory (change drives first by typing the drive letter followed by a colon, if necessary):

CD\SPREADST

Now, copy the file from the current directory (\SPREADST) to the \SPREADST\ORIG directory:

COPY MAYBUDGT.WK1 \SPREADST\ORIG

This command translates as "Copy the MAYBUDGT.WK1 file from the *current directory* to the \SPREADST\ORIG directory." The original file is still in the \SPREADST directory, and an exact duplicate is in the ORIG directory, safe and sound. If you want to copy the file in one step (without changing directories or drives), include the full path names:

COPY C:\SPREADST\MAYBUDGT.WK1 C:\SPREADST\ORIG

If you want to copy the file to a different disk drive, tweak the command a little:

COPY C:\SPREADSHT\MAYBUDGT.WK1 D:\GRAPHICS

What's Wrong with This Picture?

Here's a test of your COPY prowess. Suppose you want to copy all the files in a directory called \JOE to a directory called \BILL. You first change to the \JOE directory by typing

CD\JOE

What would you type next?

COPY \BILL *.*

COPY *.* \BILL

COPY \BILL*.*

BILL, GET OVER HERE!

Time's up! The answer is

COPY *.* \BILL

If you want to do everything in one step, include the full paths, and you get this:

COPY C:\JOE*.* C:\BILL

A lot more typing, isn't it? This command translates to "Copy all the files from the \JOE directory on drive C to the \BILL directory on drive C." All that typing means just more ways to go wrong, so I use the two-step method shown here.

Copying Files from a Directory to a Diskette

Suppose you need to print one of your spreadsheets on a printer that is attached to another PC. To do this, you want to copy your spreadsheet file, YEAREND.WK1, from the \SPREADST directory to a diskette. Then copy the file from that diskette to the other PC.

Here are the two commands that accomplish the first part of this task:

**CD\SPREADSHT
COPY YEAREND.WK1 A**

This COPY command translates to "Copy the file YEAREND.WK1 from the current directory to drive A." If you want to copy the file in one step, include the complete path names, as in

COPY C:\SPREADSHT\YEAREND.WK1 A:

Copying Files from a Diskette to a Directory

The following command translates as "Copy the file YEAREND.WK1 from the current drive to the 123 directory on the drive C."

**A:
COPY YEAREND.WK1 C:\123**

If you want to copy all the files from one diskette to another diskette *that is the exact same size and density*, you can use the DISKCOPY command. Refer to Chapter 13 for more details.

Copying Files from One Diskette to Another

If your PC has two diskette drives, copying files from one diskette to another is easy. Suppose you have a file called SALES.DOC on a 5 1/4-inch diskette and you want to copy that file to a 3 1/2-inch diskette so you can use that file on a different PC. Start by changing to drive A, then copy the file:

**A:
COPY SALES.DOC B:**

A Rose by Any Other Name: How to Give Files a Better ~~Smell~~ Spell

By now, you're probably pretty accustomed to the COPY command. If you want to make a duplicate of a file, use the COPY command, as in

COPY SALES.DOC SALES.DUP

When you rename a file, you don't create a copy of a file (as you do with the COPY command); you simply change the file name. Let's say that you want to rename a file called SALES.DOC to something more descriptive, such as APRSALES.DOC. Use this command:

REN SALES.DOC APRSALES.DOC

This command translates to "Rename the file SALES.DOC in the current directory to APRSALES.DOC."

By the Way . . .

The error **Duplicate file name or file not found** will appear if you try to rename a file to the same name as another file. Files with the same names cannot exist in the same directory, so choose another name, or move the file to another directory, as explained later in this chapter.

Get a Move On!

For years, DOS users complained about the fact that they couldn't move files. They had to copy the files into the new location and then, in a separate step, delete the files from the old location. Then came DOS 6, with the MOVE command.

If you have at least DOS 6, you can use the new MOVE command to move files in fewer steps. To use our example, you would type

CD\SPREADSHT

This changes you to the \SPREADSHT directory. Now, use the MOVE command:

MOVE INVOICES.WK1 C:\ACCTG

This command translates to "Move the INVOICES.WK1 file from the current directory to the \ACCTG directory on drive C." You can include the file path with the MOVE command to perform the move in one step:

MOVE C:\SPREADSHT\INVOICES.WK1 C:\ACCTG

This command translates to "Move the INVOICES.WK1 file from the \SPREADSHT directory on drive C to the \ACCTG directory on drive C."

How to Move Files If You Don't Have at Least DOS 6

You can still move files without DOS 6; you just have to do it the old-fashioned way: copy, then delete. For example, suppose you have a file called INVOICES.WK1 in a directory called \SPREADSHT and you want to move the file to your \ACCTG directory instead, so you can locate it easier. Use these two commands:

CD\SPREADSHT
COPY INVOICES.WK1 C:\ACCTG

These commands change you to the \SPREADSHT directory, then copy the file INVOICES.WK1 to the \ACCTG directory. The original file is still in the \SPREADSHT directory, so make sure you delete it, or you'll have two copies of the file on your hard disk:

DEL INVOICES.WK1

The DEL command removes files, as you'll learn in Chapter 11. This command translates to "Delete INVOICES.WK1 from the current directory."

Put It to Work

Creating a Batch File for Moving Files

If you don't have at least DOS 6, moving files from place to place can be a pain. To make it easier on your tired digits, create this *batch* file (which contains several commands) called MOVEFILE.BAT.

Type in exactly what you see. The DOS prompt will "disappear" for a while—but that's normal. If you make a mistake, use **Backspace** to back up and erase it. If the mistake is on a previous line, press **F6** and **Enter**, and you'll see the DOS prompt again where you can start over "at the top." (If you have at least DOS 5, and you want to learn an easier way to create and edit files, refer to Chapter 15):

```
CD\DOS
COPY CON: MOVEFILE.BAT
@ECHO OFF
IF %2!==! GOTO HELP
GOTO OK
IF NOT EXIST \%2\NUL GOTO NODIR
GOTO OK
:NODIR
ECHO.
ECHO  The directory \%2 does not exist. Move
    abandoned.
ECHO.
GOTO END
:OK
COPY %1 \%2
IF EXIST \%2\1 GOTO GOODCOPY
ECHO.
ECHO The file did not copy. Move abandoned.
ECHO.
GOTO END
DEL %1
ECHO.
ECHO The file %1 has been moved to \%2
ECHO.
:END
```

continues

continued

After you type the last line of this batch file, press **Enter**. Now press **F6** (one of those function keys at the top or left of your keyboard), and press **Enter** again. You'll see the words **1 file(s) copied**.

To use this batch file to move the file GETOUT.DOC from the current directory to the \OVERHERE directory, type this:

MOVEFILE GETOUT.DOC OVERHERE

The batch file will check to see if you've entered a directory to move the file to. Then it will copy the file to that directory and delete the original file.

The Least You Need to Know

To avoid standing at the COPY command all day, you should know these things:

- ☞ A path name consists of the drive the file is located on, a colon, a backslash, the directory path, another backslash, and the name of the file: C:\WORD\CHAP10.DOC.

- ☞ Unless you specify, DOS assumes you want to copy within the current directory. If you change to the directory first, you'll have to type less later.

- ☞ The copy command has three parts: COPY, what you're copying, and its destination. For example, COPY CONFIG.SYS CONFIG.BKP copies CONFIG.SYS to a duplicate file named CONFIG.BKP.

- ☞ To copy several files at once, use the DOS wild cards, * (which represents multiple characters) or ? (which represents a single character).

- ☞ To copy files from one directory to another, change to the source directory, then follow these examples:

COPY JOE*.* \SALES

COPY C:\MARKET\JOESALES.* C:\SALES

COPY C:\MARKET\JOESALES.WK1 D:\SALES

☞ To copy a file from a directory to a diskette, change to that directory, then follow these examples:

COPY DORPHIN.DOC A:

COPY C:\PROJECTS\DORPHIN.DOC B:

☞ To copy a file from a diskette to a directory, change to that diskette drive, then follow these examples:

COPY DORPHIN.DOC C:\WORD

COPY A:DORPHIN.DOC C:\WORD

☞ To copy files from one diskette to another, change to the source diskette, then follow these examples:

COPY SCOTTY.DOC B:

COPY A:SCOTTY.DOC B:

☞ To rename files, change to the directory that contains the files, then follow these examples:

REN BUSH.WK1 CLINTON.WK1

REN APR??MEM.DOC MAY??MEM.DOC

REN *.BAK *.OLD

☞ Unless you have at least DOS version 6, to move a file to a new directory, you must copy it from the existing directory first, then delete it, as the following sequence shows:

CD\OLD

COPY JENNY.DOC C:\NEW

DEL JENNY.DOC

☞ If you have at least DOS version 6, you can move a file in one step, as in

MOVE C:\OLD\JENNY.DOC C:\NEW

Chapter 11
Spring Cleaning— Deleting Files

In This Chapter

- ☞ Deleting a file

- ☞ Deleting all the files in a directory

- ☞ Deleting selected files

- ☞ Getting DOS to prompt you before it deletes a file

- ☞ How to recover files if you accidentally delete them

- ☞ Ways to increase your chances of recovering a deleted file

You use a PC to create things such as memos, reports, charts, and analyses. Unfortunately, PC's are not self-maintaining machines. They don't know when to take out the garbage. With the DEL command, you can clean out your PC's dust-bunnies—old files you no longer need. In this chapter, you'll learn how to use the DEL command to perform "spring cleaning" on your files. You'll also learn how to recover files if you delete them accidentally.

Things You Should Know About the DEL Command

Here's a quick review of some important concepts so you don't have to go running back to previous chapters:

Remember to press Enter to execute a command.   Until you press Enter, nothing will happen.

The DEL command is made up of two parts.   The command itself (DEL), followed by the names of the files to delete.

The DEL command deletes files without asking.   Okay, DEL will ask you "if you're crazy" when you tell it to delete all the files in the current directory—but in every other case, if you use DEL, your files are gone!

The DEL command erases files in the current directory or drive, unless you specify otherwise.   Okay, you want to delete a file, but you don't want to "get out of bed"(the directory you're currently in). Well, if you're feeling a bit sleepy—no problem. Include other directories and drives as part of the file name. For example, if you're in the WORD directory and you want to delete a file called FUN.TXT that's located in the PROJECTS directory, type **DEL C:\PROJECTS\FUN.TXT**.

When Would You Ever Want to Use the DEL Command?

When it comes to collecting stuff, I'm the Queen. I just can't seem to throw anything away (like my complete set of grocery receipts from 1983—try to replace those at today's prices). If you're like me, the mere idea of deleting any file could send you into hiding, but there are many good reasons why it's worth your while. For example, with DEL, you can

Make room for a new program.   If you're out of room, you can copy seldom-used files onto diskettes and then delete them from your hard disk (see "When Everything Must Go! How to Delete All the Files in a Directory").

Clean up a diskette for reuse.   If you have a diskette you want to recycle, you can use the DEL command to delete the files on it (see "Recycling Those Diskettes").

Get rid of files you no longer need.   If a project is over, remove the files to make more room on your hard disk (see "When Everything Must Go! How to Delete All the Files in a Directory" and "Deleting, Single-File Style").

Clean up after programs.   Many programs create working *backups* of your files. In case of a power outage, the programs use these backups to retrieve your data. These files usually end in .BAK, and they are not deleted. To make more room on your hard disk, you should periodically delete these space wasters. (See the Put It to Work project toward the end of this chapter.)

Removing an old directory.   If you need to remove a program from your hard disk, you remove its directory. From time to time, you may also want to remove personal directories that you had set up for special projects long since past. To remove a directory, it must be empty of files (see "When Everything Must Go! How to Delete All the Files in a Directory"). You'll learn how to remove the directory itself in Chapter 11.

Deleting, Single-File Style

To delete a file, you use the DEL command. For example, suppose you want to delete a file called 92PROD.CHT, located in the \CHART directory. Use these commands:

CD\CHART
DEL 92PROD.CHT

The first command changes you to the \CHART directory, and the next command deletes the file—easy as pie.

By the Way . . .

I prefer to change to the directory where the files I want to delete are stored, then use the DEL command to delete them. I find this much easier than trying to perform DEL in one step, which I could have done with this command:

DEL C:\CHART\92PROD.CHT

This command tells DOS to "Delete the 92PROD.CHT file, which is located in the \CHART directory on drive C." By including the path to the file, you can delete files in one step, although the command will be rather long (and pretty tiring on your fingers).

You might get the error message **Access denied** when using the DEL command. If you get this error message, it means that the file is protected, so you can't delete it in the normal way. Ask a PC guru to help you delete it (and to help you decide whether the file *should* be deleted).

When Everything Must Go! How to Delete All the Files in a Directory

If you want to remove a directory that's no longer needed, you must first remove all the files in it. Let's say that you had a directory called WALLS where you stored all the files for a big project. Now the project's completed, and you want to remove the directory. Just to be safe, copy all the files onto a diskette before you delete them, in case you ever need them again. So you don't have to return to Chapter 10 to remember how to copy files, here are the steps:

        CD\WALLS
        COPY *.* A:

These two commands will copy all the files in the \WALLS directory onto the diskette in drive A (provided they will all fit).

Now, to tear the walls down (as it were), use these two commands:

        CD\WALLS
        DEL *.*

When you delete all the files in a directory by using *.* (asterisk period asterisk), DOS will ask you to confirm that you haven't lost your mind and that you *really truly* want to delete everything in this directory. Press **Y** for yes, and the files are deleted. (Press **N** if you made a mistake and you don't want to delete the files.)

If you have at least DOS version 4, you can delete all the files in a directory in one step, as in

        DEL C:\WALLS

Press **Y**, and then press **Enter** to delete all the files.

Recycling Those Diskettes

Rather than buy new diskettes all the time, recycle 'em like I do. Delete all the existing files on a diskette in drive A with these two commands:

```
A:
DEL *.*
```

The first command will change you to drive A (so there's no possibility that you'll delete files on you hard disk, make sure you always check your DOS prompt to be sure that you made it to drive A). The next command deletes all the files on the diskette. Recycling diskettes in this way will only work if no one got fancy and placed directories on the diskette (it's pretty rare that you'll find directories on a diskette; they're relatively small compared to hard disks, so why bother?). If that's the case, just reformat the diskette—it's easier than trying to remove directories.

By the Way . . .

Even after you delete all the files in a directory, when you use the DIR command to list files, you'll see something like this:

```
Directory of C:\WALLS
.          <DIR>   03-20-93   3:51p
..         <DIR>   03-20-93   3:51p
     2 file(s)        0 bytes
            16957440 bytes free
```

The . (dot) represents the address of this directory, and .. (double dot) represents the address of the parent directory (which in this case is the root). Think of these as "bread crumbs" that DOS uses to find its way through the directory tree. These markers will not be removed until the directory itself is deleted, so don't worry about them.

The DEL Command Goes Wild! (Deleting Selected Files)

Use DOS *wild cards* to delete selected files in a directory. DOS has two wild cards, the asterisk (which represents several characters within a file name, as in *.DOC) and the question mark (which represents a single character within a file name, as in PART??.DOC).

For example, suppose you want to delete all your 1992 files from the SALES directory. Follow these steps:

CD\SALES
DEL 92*.*

This command deletes all the files in the current directory that begin with the numbers 92. Use wild cards in place of file names in any DEL command to delete multiple files at once.

When using wild cards to delete files, use the DIR command first to verify that you will delete the correct files. For example, to delete all the files in the current directory that begin with an M and use an .XLS extension, use this command first:

DIR M*.XLS

You'll see a listing of all the .XLS files in the current directory. If you're satisfied that the listing contains all the files you want to delete, use the DEL command with the same wild cards:

DEL M*.XLS

If the wild-card pattern lists most of the files you want, you can request confirmation for each file before it is deleted. See the next section for details.

Put It to Work
Deleting Old Backup Files

A lot of programs create working backups of your files, which they use in case a power outage has damaged your original file and made it inaccessible. These files usually end in .BAK or .TMP, and they are never deleted. To make more room on

> your hard disk, you should periodically delete them. To delete backup files from a directory called WORD, use these commands:
>
> **CD\WORD**
> **DEL *.BAK**
> **DEL *.TMP**

If you have at least DOS 5, you can search for all the backup files on your hard disk, and print out the listing, so you can go back and delete them:

DIR C:*.BAK /S >PRN

What's Wrong with This Picture?

Jorge wants to delete all his Corbitt project files. The files are in a directory called \PROJECTS, but they are mixed in with other project files. Some of the files begin with the letters COR, while others include a date, as in 0320CB.DOC, 0413CB.DOC, and 021CB.DOC. Jorge thought he'd use these commands to delete the files. What's wrong with this picture?

DEL *COR.DOC
DEL ????CB.DOC

If you said, "The problem with the first command is that it's really like saying *.DOC, which is going to delete all the .DOC files in this directory," then you'd be right. If you use an asterisk as a wild card, all the letters to the right are ignored until you bump into the period. So *COR.DOC is really *.DOC.

If you have at least DOS version 4, you can train DOS to "sit up and beg" before it deletes a file. Going back to an earlier scenario, if you want to confirm the deletion of each 1992 file, use this command instead:

DEL 92*.* /P

The /P switch tells DOS to prompt for confirmation before deleting each file. You can use the /P switch whenever you use the DEL command, but it's especially helpful when you're deleting selected files. As the name of each file appears, simply press **Y** to delete the file, or **N** to skip deletion.

What about the second command—can you see what's wrong? If you said, "Using four question marks will only get rid of the files like 0413CB.DOC, but not 021CB.DOC," you're right again. This is what Jorge should have typed:

DEL COR*.DOC
DEL ????CB.DOC
DEL ???CB.DOC

The first command deletes all the files that begin with the letters COR. The second command deletes files with four-digit dates, as in 0320CB.DOC. The third command deletes files with three-digit dates, as in 113CB.DOC.

Oops, I Deleted the Wrong Files!

If you get trigger-happy with the DEL command, it's easy to accidentally delete the wrong file. Then what do you do? Well, if you have a copy of the file on a diskette, you can easily copy it back onto your hard disk. But what do you do if you don't have a recent copy of the file, and you're out of tissues?

If you have DOS 5 or DOS 6, you have something better than tissues; you have the UNDELETE command. Suppose you have just typed the command

DEL APR93.WK1

when your boss asks you to do a comparison between last month's sales (April) and this month's. How do you get that file back? Easy—just use this command:

UNDELETE APR93.WK1

How can you recover a *deleted* file? Well, DOS doesn't actually delete a file even when you tell it to. Instead, it marks a file as "deleted" by replacing the first character in the file name with a question mark, as in

?PR93.WK1

Think of putting an "X" through an old address in your address book. You know to ignore the address, and you may even reuse that address area by placing a label over it. When DOS marks a file with a question mark, it knows not to list that file when you use the DIR command. DOS also knows that it can reuse the space at any time. For all intents and purposes, the file is deleted, but in reality, it's still there—it's simply waiting to be overwritten by another file as soon as that file needs the space. That's why it is important to use the UNDELETE command as soon as possible, to ensure your best chances of a successful recovery.

When you use the UNDELETE command, you might be asked to supply the first letter of the file name, as in

?PR93.WK1
Please supply the missing letter:

Enter the missing letter (in this case, the letter **A**) and press **Enter**. The file should be recovered. I say should be, because this command works best if you use it right after deleting the file. Don't copy files onto your hard drive or use any programs until you've recovered the deleted file. In short, *if you accidentally delete a file, do nothing until you use the UNDELETE command.*

Recovering Several Files at Once

Okay, so you deleted not one, but several files. What do you do now? Use this command:

UNDELETE /LIST

The /LIST switch displays a listing of all the recently deleted files, along with their chances of a successful recovery.

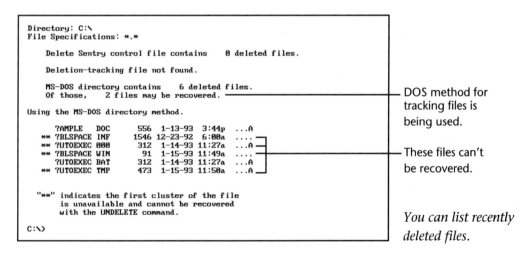

```
Directory: C:\
File Specifications: *.*

    Delete Sentry control file contains      0 deleted files.

    Deletion-tracking file not found.

    MS-DOS directory contains     6 deleted files.
    Of those,     2 files may be recovered.

Using the MS-DOS directory method.

    ?AMPLE    DOC      556  1-13-93   3:44p  ...A
 ** ?BLSPACE  INF     1546 12-23-92   6:00a  ....
 ** ?UTOEXEC  000      312  1-14-93  11:27a  ...A
 ** ?BLSPACE  WIN       91  1-15-93  11:49a  ....
    ?UTOEXEC  BAT      312  1-14-93  11:27a  ...A
 ** ?UTOEXEC  TMP      473  1-15-93  11:50a  ...A

  "**" indicates the first cluster of the file
       is unavailable and cannot be recovered
       with the UNDELETE command.

C:\>
```

DOS method for tracking files is being used.

These files can't be recovered.

You can list recently deleted files.

To undelete several files, use wild cards, as in

UNDELETE *.BAK

Increasing Your Chances of a Successful Recovery

If you don't undelete a file right after accidentally deleting it, you may not be able to get that file back. You can *greatly* increase your chances by using one of these delete protection methods:

MIRROR   Use the MIRROR command with DOS 5. MIRROR keeps a list of recently deleted files, including the location of each part of the file.

TECHNO NERD TEACHES

Often DOS stores files by breaking them into chunks and storing them in the first available spots, all over the hard disk. If a file was stored in pieces, UNDELETE will have a harder time recovering the file unless you use MIRROR, Delete Tracker, or Delete Sentry. When a file is deleted, DOS remembers where the starting piece of a file is located, but it may not remember where the rest of the pieces are. The delete protection methods listed here keep track of the exact location of each piece of a file and provide the missing information to DOS.

Delete Tracker   Use Delete Tracker with DOS 6. Delete Tracker uses less disk space than Delete Sentry, and uses a method similar to MIRROR for tracking deleted files.

Delete Sentry   Use Delete Sentry with DOS 6. Delete Sentry creates a hidden directory called \SENTRY. When you delete files, they are moved to this directory before they are deleted by DOS. When you activate UNDELETE, they are moved back to their original directory. Files are saved in this directory until the \SENTRY directory has grown to 7% of your hard disk space, then old files are deleted to make way for new ones.

Delete protection is a little tricky, so have a friend help you place the appropriate command for MIRROR, Delete Tracker, or Delete Sentry in your AUTOEXEC.BAT file.

The Least You Need to Know

De-leting files is de-lightful when you remember these things:

- ☞ To delete a single file, change to the directory that contains the file, then type **DEL** followed by the file name.

- ☞ To delete multiple files, use wild cards, as in **DEL MAR*.CHT**.

- ☞ To delete files without changing directories, include the directory in the file path, as in **DEL C:\HG\MAR*.CHT**.

- ☞ For added security, add the **/P** switch to the DEL command, so DOS will prompt you before it deletes a file (you must have at least DOS version 4 to use this).

- ☞ To recover a deleted file, use the UNDELETE command (you must have at least DOS 5). Type **UNDELETE** followed by the name of the file you want to recover.

- ☞ If you have DOS 5, increase your chances of recovering a file by using the MIRROR command in your AUTOEXEC.BAT file. If you have DOS 6, use Delete Sentry or Delete Tracker.

Chapter 12
Directory Assistance

In This Chapter

- How to change directories
- Listing the directories on a drive
- Adding new directories
- Deleting old directories
- Renaming directories
- Moving files from one directory to another

You use directories to organize your files, just as you might use shelves to organize books. You'll have a directory for every program you use, such as a word processor or a spreadsheet program. But you should create your own directories, too. After all, you're the one who'll have to locate the files when you need them. If you just snagged the Bosco account, you could create a BOSCO directory, where you'll put all the files that you generate.

Why should you bother to organize your files? For the same reason that you organize other things in your life—so you can find them when you need them, and not after a time-wasting search. And when Mr. Bosco asks about that proposal, you won't have to avoid his questions while you search for the file.

This chapter is all about directories: how to create them and how to remove them. You'll also learn how to move files around, so that you can always locate whatever you need, when you need it.

Things You Should Know About the Commands in This Chapter

So you don't have to keep thumbing back to previous chapters, here's a quick review of some important concepts:

Remember to press Enter to execute a command.   Until you press Enter, nothing will happen.

The MD (make directory) command creates a subdirectory off the current directory or drive, unless you specify otherwise.   You can include other directories and drives as part of the command. For example, if you are in the root directory, and you want to create a subdirectory for the \WORD directory and call it PROJECTS, you can type **C:\WORD\PROJECTS.**

You might get the error message Invalid path, not directory, or directory not empty when using the RD (remove directory) command.   In order to remove a directory, you must delete its files. If you get this error message, it means that the directory still has files or subdirectories in it. Follow the instructions later in this chapter for removing directories with success.

When Should You Use the Commands in This Chapter?

Let's face it—directories are borrrring! So you're probably wondering, "Should I bother to organize directories?" Well, here are some reasons why you might like to:

The TREE command helps you become acquainted with a new PC.   Find out what directories are out there on your PC's hard disk— and, by association, what programs are installed (see "Off to See the World: Finding Out What Directories You Have").

The MD (make directory) command organizes your files so you can work with them easily.   By creating directories for your own files, you can easily locate them. For example, I have a directory called \PROJECTS, and I create a subdirectory for each book I write (see "Remodeling: Adding New Directories").

The RD (remove directory) command helps you reclaim your hard disk space. To remove a program from your hard disk, you remove its directory. From time to time, you may also want to remove personal directories that you had set up for special projects long since past (see "Demodeling: Deleting Directories").

Getting things the way you like them. Whenever you move into a new office or cubicle, it's instinctive to put your "stuff" out first, to make the place "yours." Using a PC every day, you will want to customize it to the way you work. Part of that process entails creating directories that you need for your own projects and work habits, and renaming existing directories so they become meaningful (see "Remodeling: Adding New Directories" and "Renaming a Directory with DOS 6").

Changing Directories—
A Review

Why do you need to change directories? Because each program is in its own directory, you will change from one directory to another directory whenever you use different programs. So you don't have to go running back to Chapter 6, here's a review on how to change directories.

Subdirectory Actually, all directories could be considered *sub*directories, because all directories are subordinate to the one and only root directory. However, the term subdirectory is usually used to describe a directory within another directory.

To change directories, simply type the command **CD** followed by a backslash (\) and the name of the directory you want to change to. For example, to change to the WORD directory, use this command:

CD\WORD

To change to the DORPHIN directory, which is a *subdirectory* of the PROJECTS directory, use this command:

CD\PROJECTS\DORPHIN

To change to the root directory, don't enter a directory name:

CD

Quick Trick for Changing Directories

You can move one level up the directory tree by using the command

CD..

If you were in the C:\PROJECTS\DORPHIN directory, using the command CD.. would change you to its parent directory, which in this case is C:\PROJECTS. If you used the command again, you would move up one more level, to the root directory (C:\).

Off to See the World: Finding Out What Directories You Have

When I was a kid and I wanted to see what was going on in my neighborhood, I'd climb a tree and then I could see for miles. If you want to see what's going on in your PC's "neighborhood," you use the TREE command. The TREE command lists all the directories on a single drive, such as drive C.

The TREE command is useful when you're trying to organize files so you can locate them more quickly. At my old job, I inherited someone's old PC, so I used the TREE command to tell me what programs were on the PC (because each program gets its own directory) and what kind of directory structure had been set up for storing files. To display all the directories on drive C, use this command:

TREE C:\ | MORE

This command translates to "Display all the directories on drive C, beginning with the root directory, one screenful at a time." The TREE command will display the directory listing and keep on going, unless you also use the | MORE command. The character in front of the MORE command is called a *pipe character*. Just as a water pipe controls the flow of water, the pipe character (|) controls the flow of information through it.

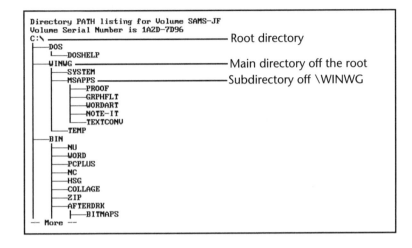

```
Directory PATH listing for Volume SAMS-JF
Volume Serial Number is 1A2D-7D96
C:\                                        ── Root directory
├──DOS
│   └──DOSHELP
├──WINWG ─────────────────────────── Main directory off the root
│   ├──SYSTEM
│   ├──MSAPPS ─────────────────────── Subdirectory off \WINWG
│   │   ├──PROOF
│   │   ├──GRPHFLT
│   │   ├──WORDART
│   │   ├──NOTE-IT
│   │   └──TEXTCONV
│   └──TEMP
├──BIN
│   ├──NU
│   ├──WORD
│   ├──PCPLUS
│   ├──NC
│   ├──HSG
│   ├──COLLAGE
│   ├──ZIP
│   ├──AFTERDRK
│   │   └──BITMAPS
── More ──
```

You can use the TREE command to list all the directories on a single disk drive, such as drive C.

The TREE command lists directories beginning with the current directory, unless you specify otherwise (as we did). Suppose you want to list all the subdirectories of your \PROJECT directory. Use a command like this one:

TREE C:\PROJECTS | MORE

What If I Want to See Files, Too?

The TREE command normally lists only directories, but you can also use it to list files (like the DIR command). Use this command to list all the files and directories on drive C:

TREE C:\ /F | MORE

The /F switch tells the TREE command to list files in addition to directories. Such a list can be used for a thorough housekeeping of your hard disk or for locating an errant file. You can't go back and forth through the list while it's displayed on-screen, so you may want to print it out:

TREE C:\ /F > PRN

Redirection symbol Used to send the output of a command to another device, a file, or another command, instead of displaying the output on the monitor. The DOS redirection symbol is the greater-than sign (>), and it is placed by the name of the device, file, or command you want to direct the output to, like this:

TREE C:\ /F > PRN

or this:

TREE C:\ > TREE.LST

The greater-than sign (>) is the *redirection symbol;* PRN is DOS's name for your printer.

You can also send the tree listing to a file, so you can save it permanently or print it out later. Use a command like this one:

TREE C:\ > TREE.LST

Remodeling: Adding New Directories

It's a good habit to keep your own files in directories other than the program directory. This makes it easier to back up your files (copy them onto diskettes in case the originals get damaged) and locate files in a hurry. For example, if your word processor is located in a directory called \WORD, you might want to create subdirectories for each project, such as \WORD\BERG and \WORD\CONFRNCE, or a single subdirectory for all the files you create, such as \WORD\PROJECTS.

To create directories, you use the MD (make directory) command. For example, let's say that you just got assigned a big account called MAYPRO, and you want to create a new directory within your WORD directory for it. Use these commands:

CD\WORD
MD MAYPRO

The first command changes you to the \WORD directory. The last command creates a subdirectory called MAYPRO within the current directory (WORD). Notice that in the example, there is no backslash in front of MAYPRO. By leaving the backslash out, *the new directory is created as a subdirectory of the WORD directory, just like you wanted.* If you had used a backslash, as in MD \MAYPRO, the MAYPRO directory would be created off the root directory, and not under the \WORD directory.

Demodeling: Deleting Directories

After you are finished with certain projects, you may not want to keep them on your hard disk. After all, they take up space that you'll need for new projects. Suppose you are finished with the MAYPRO account, and you want to delete its directory. To delete a directory, you must first delete all the files in it.

You can create directories in one step by including the complete path, as in

MD C:\WORD\MAYPRO

Make Sure You Save Those Files Before You Delete Them!

Before you delete files, you may want to copy them onto a diskette. Use these two commands:

> CD\WORD\MAYPRO
> COPY *.* A:

The first command takes you to the MAYPRO directory. The last command copies all the files in the MAYPRO directory to a diskette in drive A (provided there's enough room—if there isn't, use the BACKUP command described in Chapter 14 instead).

Be careful when deleting directories. You will not be able to recover deleted files (as described in Chapter 11) from a directory that's been removed. So make copies of any important files before you delete a directory.

Now Get Rid of That Ol' Directory!

When your files are safely copied onto diskette, you can feel comfortable deleting them. Assuming that you're still in the MAYPRO directory, use this command to delete the files:

> DEL *.*

If you get the error message **Invalid path, not directory, or directory not empty,** you either typed the path to the directory incorrectly, or the directory is not empty. All files must be removed from a directory, *along with any subdirectories,* before a directory can be removed. Use the DIR command to list the files in the directory. If you see a subdirectory (identified by the <DIR> notation), follow these steps to remove it first, then come back and remove the parent directory.

Press **Y** to confirm the deletion. Now that the directory is empty, you can remove it with the RD (remove directory) command. But first, you have to get out of the directory, too. Change to the root directory by typing

  CD\

Now, remove the directory:

  RD \WORD\MAYPRO

Why do you have to change from the MAYPRO directory before you can delete it? If you think of directories as rooms and files as boxes, then imagine that you want to remove a room of your house (maybe you're remodeling). If everything in the room was boxed up, you'd remove the boxes first. Then when you were sure that everything was out of the room, you'd remove yourself, and release the wrecking ball. Removing directories follows this same sequence: remove the files, remove yourself by changing directories, then remove the directory (the empty room).

Deleting a Directory That Contains Subdirectories

Deleting a directory that contains subdirectories is not easy, unless you have at least DOS version 6 (see the next section). But for those of us who haven't upgraded to DOS 6 yet, here's a step-by-step plan for removing a directory and its subdirectory.

Let's say that you have a directory called \OLIVE and it contains one subdirectory called \OLIVE\OIL. Removing the \OLIVE directory could get slippery, but here goes:

  CD\OLIVE\OIL
  DEL *.*

These two commands move you to the subdirectory OIL, and delete its files. Now try these two commands:

CD..
DEL *.*

The first command moves you to the parent directory, which in this case is \OLIVE. The second command deletes all the files there. Now type this:

RD \OLIVE\OIL

This command removes the subdirectory OIL. Now the directory \OLIVE is completely free of all subdirectories and files, so you can remove it, too:

CD..
RD \OLIVE

The first command moves you to the parent directory, which in this case is the root directory. The second command removes the directory \OLIVE.

Put It to Work

Creating a Batch File to Remove a Directory with Subdirectories

If you don't have DOS 6, removing directories is not fun, unless you create a simple batch file (called REMOVE.BAT) to help you.

Type in exactly what you see. The DOS prompt will "disappear" for a while—but that's normal. If you make a mistake, use **Backspace** to back up and erase it. If the mistake is on a previous line, press **F6** and **Enter**, and you'll see the DOS prompt again where you can start over "at the top." (If you have at least DOS 5 and you want to learn an easier way to create and edit files, refer to Chapter 16.)

continues

continued

```
CD\DOS
COPY CON:REMOVE.BAT
ECHO You are about to remove the %1 directory.
IF %2!==! ECHO This directory contains no
subdirectories.
IF NOT %2!==! ECHO Subdirectories to delete:
%2 %3 %4 ECHO.
ECHO If this is not correct, press Ctrl+C now.
Otherwise,
PAUSE
CD\%1
DEL *.*
IF %2!==! GOTO END
CD %2
DEL *.*
CD..
RD %2
IF %3!==! GOTO END
CD %3
DEL *.*
CD..
RD %3
IF %4!==! GOTO END
CD %4
DEL *.*
CD..
RD %4
:END
CD..
RD %1
ECHO.
ECHO The directory %1 is now gone!
ECHO.
```

After you type the last line of this batch file, press **Enter**.
Now press **F6** (one of those function keys at
the top or left of your keyboard), and press **Enter** again.
You'll see the message **1 file(s) copied**. To use this batch
file to remove the directory \OLD, which contains two
subdirectories, ONE and TWO, then
type this:

REMOVE OLD ONE TWO

You must name each subdirectory as part of the command. The batch file will delete any directory that contains up to three subdirectories.

Deleting a Directory the Easy Way— With DOS 6

If you have DOS 6, you can delete a directory in one easy step, by using the DELTREE command. The DELTREE command will automatically remove all files and sub-directories in order to remove the directory specified. For example, if you want to delete the MAYPRO directory, copy the files onto a diskette (as explained earlier) and then use this one command:

If you see the error message **Bad command or file name,** you need to set up a DOS path so that DOS can find the DELTREE or MOVE commands. See Chapter 4 for more details.

> DELTREE C:\WORD\MAYPRO

You will be prompted to confirm this deletion. Press **Y** and **Enter**, and away it goes!

Renaming a Directory with DOS 6

There may be times when you'll want to change the name of a directory. Maybe you didn't get the name right and you keep forgetting what the directory is for, or maybe the purpose of the directory has changed. Unfortunately, the good folks at Microsoft didn't think to provide you with an easy way to do this (until DOS 6). You'd think that you should use the REN command to rename directories, just as you use it to rename files, but if you try, you'll get an error message because DOS just doesn't understand. The good news is if you have at least DOS version 6, you can rename a directory with the MOVE command. For example, to rename a directory called \1992 to \1993, use this command:

> MOVE C:\1992 C:\1993

What If I Don't Have DOS 6?

If you don't use DOS 6, don't give up hope. First, create the new directory:

MD \1993

Then copy all the files from the old directory to the new directory:

CD\1992
COPY *.* \1993

Now, delete all the files in the old directory:

DEL *.*
Y

If the directory you are trying to rename contains subdirectories, it may not be worth your trouble to try to rename the directory, because it becomes more difficult to copy all the files and then delete them. Ask a pro to help you, or simply live with the current directory name.

The Least You Need to Know

I must confess, I love creating directories. When I was little, I had several cubbyholes where I'd stash my secret stuff. Now my treasure boxes are special directories I create for each project. You'll have no trouble creating and removing your own "treasure boxes" if you remember these things:

☞ To list all the directories on a drive, use the TREE command.

☞ To list all the files as well as all the directories on a drive, use the TREE command with the /F switch.

☞ To print the results of a command, add >PRN to the end of the command, as in **TREE C:\ /F >PRN**.

☞ To create a directory, type MD followed by the directory path.

☞ To delete a directory, if you do not have at least DOS 6, save any files you need onto diskette. Then change to the directory you want to delete, and delete all the files by using **DEL *.***. Next, change to the parent directory and use the RD command to remove the directory.

☞ If a directory contains a subdirectory, delete all the files in the subdirectory first, then remove the subdirectory by using the RD command. When all subirectories are removed, delete the files from the parent directory, then remove it with the RD command.

☞ If you have at least DOS 6, use the DELTREE command to remove a directory and all of its subdirectories.

☞ If you have at least DOS 6, use the MOVE command to rename a directory.

☞ If you don't have at least DOS 6, rename a directory by first creating a directory with the new name. Then copy all the files from the old directory to the new directory. Finally, delete all the files from the old directory and remove it.

Chapter 13
Can I Get That to Go?— Working with Diskettes

In This Chapter

- ☛ Preparing diskettes for use
- ☛ Performing a quick format of a diskette
- ☛ Unformatting a diskette
- ☛ Creating an emergency diskette
- ☛ Copying diskettes
- ☛ Displaying information about a disk

They don't slice, they don't dice, but they're great for leveling off lopsided office furniture. Used in a more conventional manner, diskettes are handy for storing backups of important files. Diskettes also provide an easy way to transport files to a co-worker's PC for printing or sharing. In this chapter, additional uses of diskettes are covered: as a means of restarting your system after a failure, and as a backup for irreplaceable program disks.

What Ya Gotta Know About the Commands in This Chapter

If you've just tuned in to our show, here's an update:

Remember to press Enter to execute a command.   Until you press Enter, nothing will happen.

If you have an older DOS version, you should be especially careful when using the FORMAT command.   Be sure to include a drive letter to format, or you may accidentally format your hard disk if you are not careful (this would be a really, really baaaad thing).

The most common error message you might get when using these commands is Bad command or file name.   If you get this error message, you need to set up a DOS path so that DOS can find the command. See Chapter 4 for more details.

Why Our Critics Give These Commands Two Thumbs Up

"I laughed, I cried, I formatted diskettes."

"These are the best commands you'll use in this chapter!"

"This chapter changed my life. I can't wait 'til Diskettes, Part II!"

Here's a sneak preview of when you'll need this chapter:

Using new diskettes.   Sorry, gotta format them first, unless you bought preformatted diskettes, you clever person, you (see "A Dirty Job, but Somebody's Gotta Do It: Preparing a Diskette for Use").

Formatting a diskette with a low-density diskette in a high-density drive.   Although this is not recommended, sometimes "ya gotta do what ya gotta do"—for example, if you need to transfer files from your PC to a PC with a lower-density drive (see "Formatting a Double-Density Diskette in a High-Density Drive").

Reusing a diskette.   One way to erase the files on an existing diskette is to reformat it (see "Performing a Quick Format").

Preparing for the worst.   Creating an emergency diskette will prepare you in case you encounter a problem when starting your PC (see "Calling 911: Creating an Emergency Diskette").

Protecting your investment.   After you buy a new program, you should copy the program diskettes so you'll have a backup in case something happens to them (see "Copying Diskettes").

Checking the integrity of a disk. CHKDSK can be used on diskettes to see if they have problems, but it's also an important command that you should use periodically to keep your hard drive running efficiently and avoid unnecessary problems (see "To Err Is Common: Checking Your Disks").

A Dirty Job, but Somebody's Gotta Do It: Preparing a Diskette for Use

Diskettes come in two sizes: 5 1/4-inch and 3 1/2-inch, and two types of *density*. You should buy diskettes of the same size and density as the type of diskette drive your PC comes with. Before you can use a diskette, it has to be *formatted*. Imagine printing lines on a piece of notebook paper so the person who uses it will be able to write legibly.

Although you can purchase diskettes that are preformatted, I've found that diskettes that have been formatted in the actual drive they'll be used in are more reliable.

Always be sure to type a drive letter before pressing Enter, or DOS may be tempted to format your hard disk—and you can say good-bye data! Actually, the newer DOS versions require that you enter a drive letter, to prevent you from erasing your hard disk unless you mean it. But it pays to be careful!

To format a diskette for drive A that is the same density as its drive, use the following command:

FORMAT A: /V

This command says to format a diskette in drive A to the default density of the drive and to allow you to enter an electronic volume label (that's what the /V switch is for). Although you don't need to use the /V switch, I like to label my diskettes both "inside and out." When you use the DIR command, as in

DIR A:

you'll see a listing of files, along with the volume label. If you use good descriptions, you'll be able to quickly identify the diskette—even if the paper label has fallen off!

After you type this command, you'll see a message telling you to insert the diskette into its drive. When you are ready, press **Enter** to continue.

After the diskette has been formatted, you'll be asked to enter a *volume label* (remember, that's what the /V switch is for). You may use up to 11 characters, including spaces, or press **Enter** if you don't want to label your disk. After a summary is displayed, you'll be asked if you want to format another diskette of the same density. Press **Y** or **N**, then **Enter**.

This won't display unless you have at least DOS 5. ──────

Enter volume label here. ──┐

Total space on diskette ──────

After a diskette has been formatted, a summary is displayed.

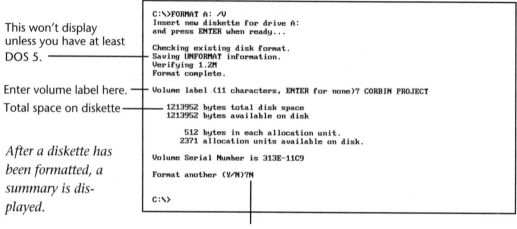

```
C:\>FORMAT A: /V
Insert new diskette for drive A:
and press ENTER when ready...

Checking existing disk format.
Saving UNFORMAT information.
Verifying 1.2M
Format complete.

Volume label (11 characters, ENTER for none)? CORBIN PROJECT

   1213952 bytes total disk space
   1213952 bytes available on disk

       512 bytes in each allocation unit.
      2371 allocation units available on disk.

Volume Serial Number is 313E-11C9

Format another (Y/N)?N


C:\>
```

Enter Y to format a similar diskette.

The diskette summary tells you how much room is on the diskette and whether there are any bad sectors (bad spots) on the diskette. You can still use a diskette with bad sectors, but you should not copy irreplaceable data on it.

You can use a diskette with bad sectors because those bad spots have been marked as "unusable" by the system. However, a diskette that has bad sectors typically develops more of them over time, so you may not want to use it. Also, a diskette is fairly cheap and easily replaced, so why take the chance?

As an interesting side note, a diskette with bad sectors may not actually be bad, but simply misformatted (formatted for the wrong density). See the next section for instructions on formatting a double-density diskette in a high-density drive.

Formatting a Double-Density Diskette in a High-Density Drive

You should try to use only high-density diskettes in a high-density drive. (It's their density!) However, if you need to use a double-density diskette in your drive, don't use it to store data that is irreplaceable. To format a double-density 5 1/4-inch diskette in a high-density drive, use this command (you must have at least DOS 4):

FORMAT A: /F:360 /V

If you have a DOS version less than DOS 4, use this command instead:

FORMAT A: /4 /V

To format a double-density 3 1/2-inch diskette in a high-density drive, use this command (you must have at least DOS 4):

FORMAT A: /F:720 /V

If you have a DOS version less than DOS 4, use this command instead:

FORMAT A: /N:9 /T:80 /V

SPEAK LIKE A GEEK

Formatting A process that prepares a diskette for use by creating invisible magnetic *tracks* (rings) on the surface of the diskette and dividing them into pie-shaped wedges called *sectors*. The number of tracks and sectors that a diskette is divided into determines its *density.*

Density Describes the amount of data a diskette can store. There are two kinds of densities: *high* and *double*. High-density diskettes hold at least twice as much as the same size double-density diskette.

Volume label A brief description or name for a diskette, recorded electronically on the disk itself. A volume label will display when DIR is used to list the files on the disk.

Unformatting a Diskette

If you have at least DOS 5, when a diskette is formatted, it is formatted *safely* (unless you specify otherwise). This means that file locations are erased, but the files themselves still exist on the diskette. Because of this, you can use the UNFORMAT command to "unerase" a formatted disk. (In previous DOS versions, once a diskette was formatted, the data was irretrievable.) To unformat a diskette, use this command:

UNFORMAT A:

Performing a Quick Format

If you have at least DOS 5, you can perform a quick format on a previously formatted diskette. Use this command when you want to clear old data from a diskette so you can reuse it. A quick format does everything a regular format does, but it does not check the disk for bad sectors. A quick format takes less time than a regular format. To perform a quick format, try this command:

FORMAT A: /Q /V

Calling 911: Creating an Emergency Diskette

An emergency diskette is used to boot your system when you have trouble starting your PC. An emergency diskette contains DOS, your AUTOEXEC.BAT, and your CONFIG.SYS. When your PC doesn't start properly (its startup information has been damaged somehow), simply place the emergency diskette in drive A, and restart your PC.

Here's why it works: when your PC boots (starts), it checks drive A first. If there is a diskette there, the PC boots using the information on the diskette. If not, the PC boots from the hard disk. You use your emergency diskette when the information on the hard disk becomes damaged and you can't start your PC any other way.

To create an emergency diskette (sometimes called a boot diskette), use a special variation of the FORMAT command:

FORMAT A: /S /V

The /S switch tells DOS to place a copy of the operating system on the diskette after formatting it. (The /V switch is optional, but it lets you place an electronic label on the disk—a good idea if you can't find a pen.) After formatting the diskette, copy your AUTOEXEC.BAT and CONFIG.SYS files with these two commands:

COPY C:\AUTOEXEC.BAT A:
COPY C:\CONFIG.SYS A:

> ## By the Way . . .
> Put your emergency diskette in a safe place, and make sure
> it's well marked, so you can find it when you need it. If you
> (or any close friend you con into it) ever change your
> AUTOEXEC.BAT or your CONFIG.SYS files, be sure to copy
> them onto this diskette again, to keep it current.

Copying Diskettes

Whenever you purchase a new software program, the first thing you
should do is make a copy of the original diskettes, because if something
happens to them, you're out of luck.

When you copy a diskette, you make an exact
duplicate. This is different from using the
COPY command, which simply copies files.
The DISKCOPY command copies the files and
the format of a diskette, all in one step. To
make a copy of a diskette, use one of these
commands:

You cannot use DISKCOPY
to copy a hard disk, only
diskettes.

    DISKCOPY A: A:

OR

    DISKCOPY B: B:

After you enter one of these commands, you will be prompted to insert
the *source diskette*. That's a computer term for the original diskette. Place
the original diskette in the indicated drive, and press **Enter**. When
prompted for the *target diskette* (a computer term for the disk you're using
to make a copy), place it in the indicated drive. If you're using one drive to
make the copy, you'll have to remove the source diskette first.

You may have to switch diskettes several times before you're done. When the copying process is complete, you'll be asked if you want to copy more diskettes. Because most programs nowadays come on several diskettes, answer yes by pressing **Y**. When you've copied the last diskette, answer no by pressing **N**.

If you have two diskette drives and they are the same type and density, you can save a bit of time by using this command instead:

DISKCOPY A: B:

To Err Is Common: Checking Your Disks

If you want to list the files on a disk, use the DIR command. If you want to check the status of a disk, use the CHKDSK command. Although you can use the CHKDSK command on your diskettes, it is much more important that you use the CHKDSK command every once in a while on your hard disk, to clean up after DOS. You see, when you delete a file, it's not really deleted. Instead, the reference to where that file is located is erased, and the area is marked "available." Sometimes, DOS is not as neat as it needs to be, and an area will be marked "used" even after the file reference is erased. This creates something called a *lost cluster* or a *lost chain*.

Lost clusters and lost chains Lost clusters and chains are pieces of files that have been "lost" by DOS. When you delete a file, it is not actually erased; instead, the reference to the file's location is erased. If a file's location is erased from the file listing but its address is still marked "used," you get a lost cluster. If several of these clusters occur together on the disk, you get a lost chain.

To clean up these lost chains and clusters, and to make that space available again, use CHKDSK. *Don't try to use CHKDSK on a network drive, such as drive F. To use CHKDSK to check the status of drive C, you must exit all programs first.* Then use this command:

CHKDSK C: /F

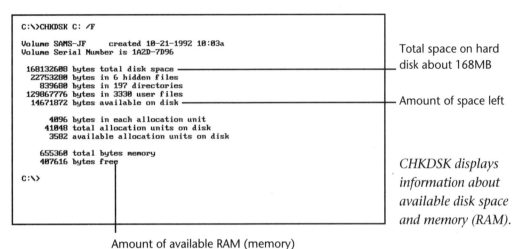

```
C:\>CHKDSK C: /F

Volume SAMS-JF     created 10-21-1992 10:03a
Volume Serial Number is 1A2D-7D96

 168132608 bytes total disk space ————————————
  22753280 bytes in 6 hidden files
    839680 bytes in 197 directories
 129867776 bytes in 3330 user files
  14671872 bytes available on disk ——————————

      4096 bytes in each allocation unit
     41048 total allocation units on disk
      3582 available allocation units on disk

    655360 total bytes memory
    407616 bytes free

C:\>
```

Total space on hard disk about 168MB

Amount of space left

CHKDSK displays information about available disk space and memory (RAM).

Amount of available RAM (memory)

If you get a message like this:

2 lost allocation units found in 1 chains.
8192 bytes disk space would be freed.

you have lost clusters or chains, so press **Y** to convert them to usable space. DOS creates a file to contain the data that was in each lost cluster. The data is probably unusable because it's part of an old file. To delete the files, use this command:

DEL C:\FILE????.CHK

If you get the message

Errors found, F parameter not specified
Corrections will not be written to disk

then you have forgotten to type /F. Retype the command and be sure to include the /F switch.

OOPS!

If you forget the /F switch, CHKDSK will pretend that it's fixing the problem, but when you run CHKDSK again, the problem will still be there. The /F switch tells DOS to write the changes to the disk.

The Least You Need to Know

Performing diskette surgery is easy if you remember these tips:

- ☛ To format a diskette that is the same density as its drive, type **FORMAT**, a space, the letter of the diskette drive to format, then a colon. You can add the switch **/V** to the command if you want to enter a volume label.

- ☛ To format a double-density 5 1/4-inch diskette in a high-density drive, use this command (you must have at least DOS 4): **FORMAT A: /F:360 /V.**

- ☛ To format a double-density 3 1/2-inch diskette in a high-density drive, use this command (you must have at least DOS 4): **FORMAT A: /F:720 /V.**

- ☛ If you have at least DOS 5, you can unformat a diskette if it was formatted by accident. Use the UNFORMAT command.

- ☛ If you have at least DOS 5, you can perform a quick format on a previously formatted diskette by including the /Q switch.

- ☛ To create an emergency boot diskette, follow these steps:

    FORMAT A: /S /V

    COPY C:\AUTOEXEC.BAT A:

    COPY C:\CONFIG.SYS A:

- ☛ To make an exact copy of a diskette, use the DISKCOPY command.

- ☛ To check any disk for disk errors such as lost clusters, use the CHKDSK command. Be sure to include the /F parameter, as in **CHKDSK C: /F.**

Part Three
Things Your PC Guru Never Told You

I hate when I'm having a computer problem, and someone says, "You mean you didn't do . . . ?" The hardest thing about using a computer is that there's always something that someone will forget to tell you. This section deals with the kinds of things you should know about, even if you don't want to do them yourself. With just a little light reading (I promise) you can prevent major, big-time problems later.

Chapter 14
Backing Up Your Hard Disk

In This Chapter

- ☞ Backing up all the files on your hard disk
- ☞ Backing up only the files you created or changed recently
- ☞ Using MS-DOS 6 to perform backups

True story: One day I was sitting at a red light, minding my own business, and suddenly I found myself on the other side of the intersection. Someone was playing road hockey, and I was the puck. When the cops arrived, they said I was lucky; I had been wearing my seat belt.

Doing *backups* is something like wearing a seat belt: it's annoying, and you wonder why you bother doing it, until an accident happens and you're glad you did. (At least a backup won't wrinkle your clothes.)

This chapter is divided into two sections: the first half is for users who don't have DOS 6, and the last half is for those who do.

If you don't know what your DOS version is, type

    VER

If you have DOS 6, the way you do backups is different from previous DOS versions, so read the section "If You've Skipped Ahead,

SPEAK LIKE A GEEK

Back up A process that copies files onto a diskette or backup tape in a special format. This process compresses the files so that more of them can be placed on a diskette or tape than by using the COPY command. By backing up important files onto a diskette or a tape, you can restore those files if the originals get damaged in some way.

BACK UP and Read This!," and then skip to the end of this chapter and read "Backing Up Your Hard Disk with DOS 6."

If You've Skipped Ahead, BACK UP and Read This!

The backup command that you use with DOS 6 is MSBACKUP. For earlier DOS versions, use MR BACKUP (okay, okay, I'm just being silly—earlier DOS versions really use the plain old BACKUP command). Now before I get too carried away, here are some important concepts you should know:

Remember to press Enter to execute a command.   Until you press Enter, nothing happens.

The backup commands are used to protect the files on your hard disk.   You cannot use BACKUP or MSBACKUP to make copies of files on diskettes.

There's a difference between COPY and the backup process.   When you copy a file to a disk, the copy is usable. When you back up a file, the backed-up version is unusable until you restore it. Another difference: when you copy a file to a disk, existing files on the disk remain. The backup procedure takes control of the whole disk and wipes out its previous contents.

SPEAK LIKE A GEEK

Full backup A type of backup that copies every file on your hard disk.

Incremental backup A type of backup that copies only the files that have been changed since the last full or incremental backup. To restore a complete hard disk, you would need *both your full and all of your incremental backup diskettes.*

There are different types of backups you can perform.   You can back up all of your files or only selected ones. It's your choice, *full* or *incremental*. As a rule of thumb, perform a full backup once a week, and then perform an incremental backup at the end of each work day.

To format or not to format.   Performing a backup uses a lot of diskettes. If you have at least DOS version 4, you don't have to preformat the diskettes used in a backup—just use them straight out of the box. BACKUP and MSBACKUP will format diskettes as needed. However, using already formatted diskettes will make the backup process go much faster.

You should check for viruses before you perform a backup. One reason why you may need these backup disks in the first place is to restore your system after a computer virus has trashed it, so make sure your backups will be usable by checking for viruses first (see Chapter 17).

Why Worry?—Backing Up the Entire Hard Disk

When I back up my entire hard disk, it gives me a feeling of euphoria. Because every file is safely copied onto a diskette, I can look my PC in the eye and say, "You can be replaced." If you have DOS 6, skip to "Backing Up Your Hard Disk with DOS 6" to find out what to do. If you have an earlier DOS version, you too can get that "Oh, what a feeling" by using this command:

> BACKUP C:*.* A: /S /L

This command tells DOS to "Back up all the files on drive C, beginning with the root directory, and create a log of all the files that are backed up." You'll be prompted to place a diskette in drive A and to replace that diskette with other diskettes until the entire hard disk is backed up. The number of diskettes needed will vary, depending on the size of your hard disk and the capacity (density) of the diskettes you're using.

Any information already on the diskettes you use in a backup will be erased, so make sure that you don't need any of the files on the diskettes.

Put It to Work

Figuring Out How Many Diskettes You'll Need to Do a Full Backup

Type this command:

CHKDSK

Take the *bytes total disk space* minus the *bytes available on disk* to find the number of bytes being used. Take this number and divide it by the number of bytes each diskette holds:

	High-Density	Double-Density
5 1/4-inch	1,258,291.2 bytes	360 bytes
3 1/2-inch	1,509,949.44 bytes	720 bytes

For example, if my PC had a total of 168,132,608 bytes (160MB) and all but 14,598,144 bytes were used, then I'd have to back up 153,534,464 bytes (yech). If I used high-density 3 1/2-inch diskettes, then the backup would take 101.68 diskettes (better make that 102 disks). Some compression occurs during backup, so this is actually an overestimate (lucky me).

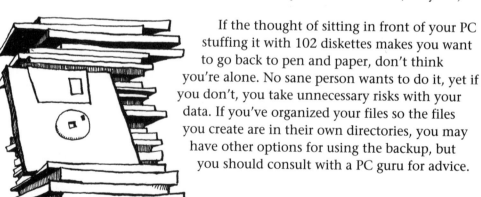

If the thought of sitting in front of your PC stuffing it with 102 diskettes makes you want to go back to pen and paper, don't think you're alone. No sane person wants to do it, yet if you don't, you take unnecessary risks with your data. If you've organized your files so the files you create are in their own directories, you may have other options for using the backup, but you should consult with a PC guru for advice.

What If I Have Another Disk Drive?

If you have more than one disk drive, such as drive D, you'll need two complete sets of backups—one set for C, the other for D. *Don't reuse the same diskettes.* Use this command to do a full backup of drive D:

BACKUP D:*.* A: /S /L

The Lazy Way—Backing Up Only What's Changed

The problem with the full backup euphoria is that as soon as you change or create a document, you need to do a backup again. Instead of doing a complete backup all over again, do an incremental one. An incremental backup backs up only those files that have changed since your last backup. For the most part, these are the files you've changed, so there shouldn't be too many of them. Use this command to perform an incremental backup of drive C:

BACKUP C:*.* A: /S /M /A /L

This command translates to "Back up all the files on drive C, beginning with the root directory, that have been modified since the last backup. Add this to the existing backup set, and update the log file." You will need to dig out your full backup set, and place diskette 1 in drive A. You'll be prompted for other diskettes in the backup set, as needed. This command updates the files on the full backup and adds any new files.

Put It to Work
Automating the Backup Process with a Batch File

Because backup commands are hard to type and easy to get wrong, create this batch file (called EZBACKUP.BAT) to help you. Note: this batch file assumes that you use drive A for your backups and that you have only one disk drive, drive C. Make the appropriate changes for your system.

continues

continued

Type everything else exactly as you see it. The DOS prompt "disappears" for a while, but that's normal. If you make a mistake, use **Backspace** to back up and erase it. If the mistake is on a previous line, press **F6** and **Enter**, and you'll see the DOS prompt again where you can start over "at the top."

```
CD\DOS
COPY CON: EZBACKUP.BAT
@ECHO OFF
FOR %%J IN (w W d D) DO IF "%1"=="%%J" GOTO OK
:HELP
CLS
ECHO.
ECHO You need to specify which type of backup to
perform.
ECHO Use W for Weekly (full backup), and D for daily
ECHO (incremental backup.)
ECHO.
ECHO To perform a weekly (full backup), type this:
ECHO.
ECHO    EZBACKUP W
ECHO.
GOTO END
:OK
FOR %%X IN (d D) DO IF "%1"=="%%X" GOTO DAILY
:WEEKLY
BACKUP C:\*.* A: /S /L
GOTO END
:DAILY
BACKUP C:\*.* A: /S /M /A /L
:END
```

If you have at least DOS 5, and you want to learn an easier way to create and edit files, refer to Chapter 16.

After you type the last line of this batch file, press **Enter**. Now press **F6** (one of those function keys at the top or left of your keyboard), and press **Enter** again. You'll see the words **1 file(s) copied**.

To use this batch file to do a weekly or full backup, type

EZBACKUP W

To use this batch file to do a daily or incremental backup, type

EZBACKUP D

Backing Up Your Hard Disk with DOS 6

The backup program that comes with DOS 6 is called MS Backup. MS Backup is graphical, like the DOS Shell. This means that you'll select the drives, directories, and files to be backed up from menus and boxes, instead of typing commands. These selections can be stored permanently in a *setup file*, so you can reuse them at a later date. MS Backup comes with a few setup files already created for common situations, such as a full backup.

When a backup is performed, a *backup catalog* is created. A backup catalog is a file that contains information about what was backed up, and when. The backup catalog is copied to both the hard disk and the last backup diskette. The backup catalog is used when restoring files.

You can use the MS Backup program with either a mouse or the keyboard. If you've forgotten these common mouse terms, here's your roll call, mouseketeers:

Click   To click with the mouse, press the mouse button once.

Double-click   To double-click with the mouse, press the mouse button twice in rapid succession.

Backing Up the Entire Hard Disk

To perform a full backup, type this command:

MSBACKUP

The first time you run MS Backup, it will run some tests on your system so it can set itself up. You will need two diskettes of the same size and density as the diskettes you'll use when you do real backups. Follow the on-screen instructions, and remember to save the configuration when the tests are over. When the testing is done, press **Enter** to select Backup from the Main menu, and you'll see the screen where you'll make all your backup selections. Next time you use MS Backup, type **MSBACKUP** and press **Enter**, and you'll get to this screen right away.

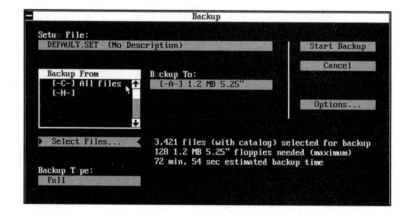

You can configure your backup from the Backup dialog box.

1. Start by selecting the drive to back up in the Backup From box. Press **Tab** until the box is highlighted, use the arrow keys to highlight a drive, and then press the **Spacebar** to select it. If you're using a mouse, click with the right mouse button on the drive to back up. MS Backup will display "All Files" next to the drive letter you select. Repeat for additional drives.

2. Change the drive to back up to, if necessary. If you are going to use diskettes of a different type or size than the one listed, change the drive letter in the Backup To box. Press **Tab** until the box is highlighted, and press **Enter** to display the selections. Use the arrow keys to select the drive, and then press **Enter**. If you're using a mouse, click on the box to display the selections, then click on the drive to use. Click on the **OK** button when you are done.

3. When you're ready to go, select Start Backup. Press **Tab** until it's highlighted and press **Enter**. If you're using a mouse, click on the Start Backup button.

Performing an Incremental or Differential Backup

As you learned earlier in the chapter, DOS lets you do either a full or an incremental backup. When you do an incremental backup, DOS backs up the files that have been changed since the last backup (of any kind). That means that if you ever need to restore your entire hard disk, you not only need the diskettes from your last full backup, but the diskettes from every incremental backup you did after it. That can be a lot of diskettes!

> **SPEAK LIKE A GEEK**
>
> **Differential backup** This backup copies only the files that have been changed since the last full backup. To restore a complete hard disk, *you would need both your full and your latest differential backup diskettes.*

MS-DOS 6 has an additional type of backup, called a *differential backup*. A differential backup saves you some disks, by backing up all the files that have been changed since the last full backup, even if they were backed up already by an incremental or differential backup. This is cool because you don't have to keep the diskettes for each differential backup you do between full backups—only the most recent one.

Performing an incremental or differential backup of your entire hard disk is easy. Start the backup process by typing

MSBACKUP

Press **Enter** with the **Backup** box highlighted, then follow these steps:

1. Start by selecting the drive to back up in the Backup From box. Press **Tab** until the box is highlighted, use the arrow keys to select a drive, then press the **Spacebar**. If you're using a mouse, click with the right mouse button on the drive to back up. MS Backup will display "All Files" next to the drive letter you select. Repeat for additional drives.

2. Change the drive to back up to, if necessary. If you are going to use diskettes of a different type or size than the one listed, change the drive letter in the Backup To box. Press **Tab** until the box is highlighted, and press **Enter** to display the selections. Use the arrow keys to select the drive, then press **Enter**. If you're using a mouse, click on the box to display the selections, then click on the drive to use. Click **OK** when you are done.

3. Select Incremental or Differential. In the Backup Type box, select the type of backup you want. Press **Tab** until the box is highlighted, and press **Enter** to display the selections. Use the arrow keys to select the backup type, then press **Enter**. If you're using a mouse, click on the Backup Type box to display the selections, then click on the backup type to use. Click on the **OK** button when you are done.

4. When you're ready to go, select Start Backup. Press **Tab** until it's highlighted and press **Enter**. If you're using a mouse, click on the Start Backup box.

The Least You Need to Know

I was a horrible Girl Scout—whenever we'd go camping, my marshmallows would act out the role of Joan of Arc, and I'd always come home with a case of poison ivy. I swear I can catch poison ivy anywhere—I once caught it on a tour through a museum! But one thing about scouting stuck, and that's "Be prepared." You will be too, if you remember these things:

- ☞ Backing up your hard disk is a process that copies files onto a diskette or a backup tape in a special format. This process compresses the files so that more of them can be placed on a diskette or a tape than by using the COPY command. By backing up important files onto a diskette or a tape, you can restore those files if the originals get damaged in some way.

- ☞ DOS versions prior to 6 support two different types of backups: full and incremental. In a full backup, all the files on the disk drive are copied onto diskettes. In an incremental backup, only the files that have been changed or created since the last backup are copied onto diskettes.

- ☞ To perform a full backup of drive C, type this command:

    BACKUP C:*.* A: /S /L

☞ To perform an incremental backup of drive C, type this command:

BACKUP C:*.* A: /S /M /A /L

☞ To perform a full backup with DOS 6, type **MSBACKUP**, and press **Enter** to display the backup screen. Select the drive to back up, change the drive to back up to, then select **S**tart Backup.

☞ To perform an incremental backup with DOS 6, type **MSBACKUP**, and press **Enter** to display the backup screen. Select the drive to back up, change the drive to back up to, then select the backup type. Then select **S**tart Backup.

Chapter 15
Restoring Your Hard Disk

In This Chapter

- Restoring all the files on your hard disk
- Restoring selected directories or files
- Asking to be prompted before a file is restored
- Using MS-DOS 6 to restore files

Okay, the worst has happened. You try to open an important document, and you're greeted with **Data error reading file**. Or worse yet, all the files on your hard disk have somehow been eaten by the latest computer virus. What do you do? Well, you thank your lucky stars that you read Chapter 14, then you just sit back, relax, and *restore* them.

This chapter is divided into two sections: the first half is for users who don't have DOS 6, and the last half is for those who do. If you have DOS 6, read the sections "This Section Should Not Be Removed Under Penalty of Law" and "Top 10 Reasons Why You'd Want to Restore Files," then skip to the end of this chapter and read "Restoring Your Hard Disk with DOS 6." If you don't know what your DOS version is type

    VER

This Section Should Not Be Removed Under Penalty of Law

Okay, here's the section that tells you all the stuff you could have learned in previous chapters but didn't, because why should you? I mean, that's what this book's for. Anyway, here's the usual list of things to know before preceding:

In DOS 6, there's one command—MSBACKUP—that lets you both back up and restore. In prior DOS versions, backing up is done with BACKUP, while restoring is done with a separate command, called (quite appropriately) RESTORE.

Remember to press Enter to execute a command. Until you press Enter, nothing happens.

The restore process restores files to a hard disk. You cannot restore files onto a diskette.

Files must be restored into the directory from which they came. If a file is backed up from the \SALES directory, you can't restore it to the \MARKETG directory. (However, you *can* restore files onto a different drive.)

There's a difference between COPY and the restore process. Backed-up files are compressed, so they're unusable until you restore them. Copied files are immediately usable.

You can perform different types of restore operations. You can restore all of your files, or only selected files or directories.

Top 10 Reasons Why You'd Want to Restore Files

David Letterman, look out!

Your hard disk is wiped out. If human error or mechanical disaster trashes all your files, restore everything (see "When Your Hard Disk Kicks the Bit Bucket").

A file becomes damaged, and is unreadable.   This happens in a number of ways: the power goes out while you're working on a document or maybe a bad spot develops on the hard disk where the file is located. You can restore a single file, or a whole directory (see "When Your Hard Disk Only Nicks the Bit Bucket" or "Restoring Selected Files and Directories").

You buy a new PC and you want to transfer your files onto it.   Back up your files from one PC and restore them to another (see "When Your Hard Disk Kicks the Bit Bucket").

All right, I only gave you three reasons, but believe me—if your files are damaged, you're not going to need ten reasons why you'd want to restore them.

When Your Hard Disk Kicks the Bit Bucket

Don't get me wrong: with utilities like Norton Utilities, PC Tools, and Mace Utilities, it's rare that your hard disk konks out so completely that you have to restore the whole thing. So before you attempt the whole process, get a PC guru to check your system first. Maybe the problem can be fixed without restoring everything.

However, this doesn't mean that you shouldn't perform backups and keep them current. Having a complete backup of your hard disk is like having accident insurance. When disaster strikes, you'll be glad you kept up your premiums. To restore your hard disk, use this command:

RESTORE A: C:*.* /S

This command tells DOS to "Restore all the files on drive C, beginning with the root directory." You'll be prompted to place the first backup diskette in drive A and to replace the diskette with other diskettes until the entire drive is restored.

What If I Have Another Disk Drive?

If you need to restore a system with more than one disk drive, you'll need to perform two restore processes—for instance, one for C, the other for D. When you backed up your system, you created a second set of backup diskettes for the extra drive. To restore drive D using the second set of backup diskettes, try this command:

RESTORE A: D:*.* /S

When Your Hard Disk Only Nicks the Bit Bucket

If you accidentally break a finger, you don't amputate your hand, you just put a splint on it. The same thing's true of your hard drive; if only a single file has been damaged, you don't have to restore an entire hard disk. Use this command to restore the file DAMAGED.DOC to your \WORD directory:

RESTORE A: C:\WORD\DAMAGED.DOC

This command tells DOS to "Restore the file DAMAGED.DOC to drive C, into the \WORD directory." You'll need to dig out your full backup set and place the requested diskette into drive A. Because large files can be split onto several diskettes, you may be prompted for other diskettes in the backup set.

Restoring a Single Directory

If you're having problems with a particular directory, you may want to restore only that directory, and any subdirectories too. Use this command to restore the \PROJECTS directory and all of its subdirectories:

RESTORE A: C:\PROJECTS*.* /S

This command tells DOS to "Restore the directory \PROJECTS on drive C, and any subdirectories."

Restoring Only the Files That Have Not Been Changed

Suppose you wanted to restore a directory, but not overlay any files that have changed since the backup was done. Follow this command to restore only unmodified files to the \PROJECTS directory:

RESTORE A: C:\PROJECTS*.* /S /M

This command tells DOS to "Restore only the files that have not been modified since the last backup to the \PROJECTS directory and all of its subdirectories." The /M switch limits the restore process to the files that have not been modified since the last backup. Files that have been deleted since the last backup will be restored also.

Sometimes It's Nice to Be Asked

To have the most control over the restoration process, you can ask to be prompted before any file is restored. Using our \PROJECTS example, here's the command:

RESTORE A: C:\PROJECTS*.* /S /P

This command translates to "Restore the \PROJECTS directory and all of its subdirectories to drive C, but prompt before restoring each file." The use of the /P switch causes a prompt to appear before any file is restored. Type a **Y** to restore a file, and an **N** to bypass it.

Restoring Your Hard Disk with DOS 6

As you may recall from the previous chapter, the backup and restore program that comes with DOS 6 is called MS Backup. You can use the MS Backup program with either a mouse or the keyboard. To "restore" your memory of how to use a mouse, here's a quick refresher:

Click   To click with the mouse, press the mouse button once.

Double-click   To double-click with the mouse, press the mouse button twice in rapid succession.

Restoring the Hard Disk and Your Sanity

To perform the full restore process, type this command:

MSBACKUP

Click on the **Restore** button, or press **Tab** until it is highlighted, and then press **Enter**. You'll see the screen where you'll make all your selections.

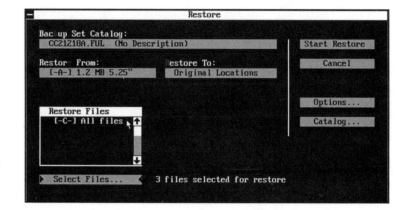

You can configure your restoration from the Restore dialog box.

1. Start by selecting the drive to restore in the Restore Files box. Set this to the drive letter that the files were originally backed up from, regardless of whether you want to restore the files to another drive. Press **Tab** until the box is highlighted, use the arrow keys to select a drive, and then press the **Spacebar**. If you're using a mouse, click with the right mouse button on the drive to restore. MS Backup will display "All Files" next to the drive letter you select. Repeat for additional drives.

2. Change the drive to restore from, if necessary. If you are going to use diskettes of a different type or size than the one listed, change the drive letter in the Restore From box. Press **Tab** until the box is highlighted, and press **Enter** to display the selections. Use the arrow keys to select the drive, and then press **Enter**. If you're using a mouse, click on the box to display the selections, and then click on the drive to use. Click on the **OK** button when you are done.

3. Change the drive to restore to, if necessary. If you want to restore files to a different drive from which they were backed up, use the **Restore To** button. Press **Tab** until the box is highlighted, and press **Enter** to display the selections. Use the arrow keys to select Other Drives or Other Directories, and then press **Enter**. If you're using a mouse, click on the box to display the selections. Then click either Other Drives or Other Directories. Click on the **OK** button when you are done.

4. When you're ready to go, select Start Restore. Press **Tab** until it's highlighted and press **Enter**. If you're using a mouse, click on the Start Restore button.

Restoring Selected Files and Directories

If only certain files or directories are damaged, you can restore only what you need. Start the restore process by typing

MSBACKUP

Press **Enter** with the **Restore** button highlighted, follow steps 1–3 in the previous section. Then follow these steps:

1. Select the file(s) to restore. Press **Tab** until the Select Files box is highlighted, then press **Enter** to display the Select Restore Files dialog box. If you are using a mouse, click on the Select Files button. Select the files or directories you want to restore. Selected directories display with an arrow. If all the files in a directory are not selected, it is displayed with a double-arrow. Selected files display with a check mark:

   Using a mouse, click with the right mouse button on any file or directory to select it. To select multiple files or directories at once, press **Ctrl** as you click on them.

   Using the keyboard, press **Tab** to move between the directory and file sections. Move the highlight with the arrow keys, then press the **Spacebar** to select an item.

2. Select **OK** to return to the Restore Window.

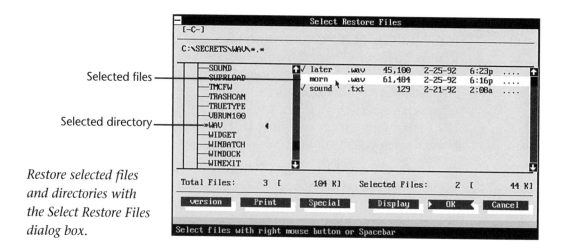

Selected files ——

Selected directory ——

*Restore selected files
and directories with
the Select Restore Files
dialog box.*

3. When you're ready to go, select **Start Restore**. Press **Tab** until it's
   highlighted and press **Enter**. If you're using a mouse, click on the
   Start Restore button.

The Least You Need to Know

When you got a sick hard disk, you want to get it "well" as
soon as possible—and you will, if you remember these
things:

☞ When you restore your hard disk, DOS copies files
from a backup diskette or tape onto your hard disk.
You perform the restore process when your original
files have been damaged in some way.

*If you don't use DOS 6, follow these instructions to restore all or
part of your hard disk:*

☞ To restore a full backup of drive C, type this command:

RESTORE A: C:*.* /S

☞ To restore a single file, such as GOODCOPY.DOC to
the directory \WORD\DOCS on drive C, type this
command:

RESTORE A:
C:\WORD\DOCS\GOODCOPY.DOC

☞ To restore a single directory, such as the \WORKS directory, and all of its subdirectories, use this command:

RESTORE A: C:\WORKS*.* /S

☞ To restore only files that have not changed since the last backup was done, use something like this:

RESTORE A: C:*.* /S /M

☞ To restore files after being prompted, use something like this:

RESTORE A: C:*.* /S /P

☞ To restore a full backup with DOS 6, start by typing this command:

MSBACKUP

Select the **R**estore button to display the restore screen. Next, select the drive to restore, change the drive to restore from, change the drive to restore to, then select **OK**. Select **S**tart Restore.

☞ To restore only selected files and directories with DOS 6, start by typing this command:

MSBACKUP

Select the **R**estore button to display the restore screen. Next, select the drive to restore, change the drive to restore from, change the drive to restore to, then select the files or directories to restore. When you're ready, select **S**tart Restore.

Chapter 16
Who, Me? Edit My Startup Files?

In This Chapter

- ☞ Easy ways to change your AUTOEXEC.BAT and CONFIG.SYS

- ☞ How to use EDIT without fear

- ☞ How to use EDLIN like a pro

- ☞ Creating simple batch files that make your life easier

Just like a car, to help your PC run at its best, you have to do a little maintenance. This includes fine-tuning your PC's engine (adjusting the AUTOEXEC.BAT and CONFIG.SYS files) so your PC runs the way you want it to. Some changes are needed to make certain programs run at their best, and others are needed to make certain programs run at all. Some programs make their own changes, while others ask you to do it. Lastly, there are some changes you'll want to make for yourself.

The bottom line is this: at one point or another, you're going to be faced with the problem of editing either your AUTOEXEC.BAT, CONFIG.SYS, or some other file (unless you're lucky enough to get somebody else to do it). In this chapter, you'll learn the most painless ways to edit your startup files.

If you have at least DOS 5, you can use EDIT, which is very simple and easy to use. EDIT is covered at the beginning of this chapter. If you don't have at least DOS 5, then you get to use a simple, but silly-looking editor called EDLIN, covered at the end of this chapter.

Pssst! Before You Edit . . .

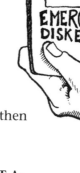

When you edit your configuration files, keep these things in mind:

☞ Do not edit CONFIG.SYS or AUTOEXEC.BAT without an emergency diskette handy. To create an emergency diskette, pop a blank diskette in drive A, then enter these commands:

Boot drive Your boot drive is the drive which contains your operating system files, usually drive C.

```
FORMAT A: /S /V
COPY C:\AUTOEXEC.BAT A:
COPY C:\CONFIG.SYS A:
```

also page 130

☞ You'll find your CONFIG.SYS and AUTOEXEC.BAT (if they exist) in the root directory of your *boot drive*.

☞ If you make changes to a configuration file, make sure you reboot your PC (press **Ctrl+Alt+Del**) to make those changes effective.

Put It to Work

Creating Your First File

If you've done any of the Put It to Work projects in earlier chapters, you've already created your first file, but you used COPY CON instead of an editor. Let's use COPY CON again, to create a fake configuration file to practice with. Type this:

```
CD\
COPY CON: FAKEEXEC.BAT
C:\DOS\SMARTDRV.EXE
SET PCPLUS=C:\PCPLUS
SET TEMP=C:\TEMP
```

> After typing the text for the file, press **F6**, then press **Enter** to close the file and save it.
>
> COPYCON works great to create a file, but it has two problems: you can't make changes to an existing file with it, and if you make a mistake, you have to start over. The two editing programs you'll learn about in this chapter, EDIT and EDLIN, overcome these difficulties.

EDIT, the Cinemascope Editor

If you have at least DOS 5, you've lucked out because it comes with an easy-to-use, full-screen text editor called EDIT. As an added bonus, there's hardly anything you need to learn in order to edit simple files such as CONFIG.SYS and AUTOEXEC.BAT.

One of the most common commands you add to your AUTOEXEC.BAT file is the PROMPT command. The PROMPT command changes the default DOS prompt from something boring like C>, to something fancy, like

C:\WORD\DOCS>

Let's add this command (and others) to a configuration file, using EDIT. We'll practice on FAKEEXEC.BAT (instead of the real AUTOEXEC.BAT); you can modify AUTOEXEC.BAT later, after you feel comfortable.

Let's Get Started

Because it's not a real configuration file, the changes you make to FAKEEXEC.BAT will not permanently change the way your computer runs. To start EDIT in order to make changes to FAKEEXEC.BAT, type this:

EDIT C:\FAKEEXEC.BAT

Our FAKEEXEC.BAT file is ready to edit.

This command tells DOS to "Start the EDIT program and open the file FAKEEXEC.BAT in the root directory of drive C." If you didn't do the FAKEEXEC.BAT project earlier, and you enter this command, DOS assumes you want to create the file. EDIT opens with a blank screen titled FAKEEXEC.BAT, which you can type the file on. (Turn back to the project to see what to type.)

If you get the error message **Bad command or file name**, you need to set up a DOS path so that DOS can find the EDIT command. You're in luck, because this is exactly the type of thing you should add to your FAKEEXEC.BAT. While we're adding our prompt, we'll add a path, too. For now, type this to start EDIT:

CD\DOS
EDIT C:\FAKEEXEC.BAT

Later, when you feel comfortable with editing, make the changes to your AUTOEXEC.BAT file, too.

EDIT Lets You Really Move

Once a file is open, you can make changes to it. Although there are many ways to move around the screen, we don't plan on being in this file long enough to care. Just to make sure, here are a few tips:

To move:	Press:
Up, down, left, or right	Arrow keys
To the beginning of a line	Home key
To the end of a line	End key

When you start the DOS 6 editor, you're in the *Insert mode*. To insert a new line, move to the beginning of the line where you want to insert and press **Enter**. If you want to type over existing characters, press the **Insert** key. You are now in *Overtype mode*. To return to Insert mode, press the **Insert** key again. If you want to delete some characters, position your cursor on any character, and use the **Delete** key.

Let's insert our two commands after the line **C:\DOS\SMARTDRV.EXE**. Move to the S in SET on line two by using the down arrow key, and press **Enter** to create a blank line. Then move up to the blank line by using the arrow key, and type this line:

    PROMPT PG

Press **Enter** to start a new line, and then type this:

    PATH=C:\DOS

The first command changes your prompt so that it displays the current drive and directory. The second command provides access to certain DOS commands like EDIT. Now the file looks like this:

    C:\DOS\SMARTDRV.EXE
    PROMPT PG
    PATH=C:\DOS
    SET PCPLUS=C:\PCPLUS
    SET TEMP=C:\TEMP

SPEAK LIKE A GEEK

Insert mode The default mode for word processors and text editors. Insert mode means that when you position your cursor and start to type, what you type is inserted at that point.

Overtype mode The opposite of Insert mode, as used in word processors and text editors. Overtype mode means that when you position your cursor and start to type, what you type replaces existing characters at that point.

OOPS!

If you accidentally create an extra blank line, move to that line and press **Delete**.

Now, for another exercise. Let's say you've re-installed the ProComm Plus program into a new directory called D:\UTILITY. You need to change the SET command to reflect this. Position the cursor to the right of the equals sign in SET PCPLUS=C:\PCPLUS, on the letter C. Press the **Insert** key, and you are in Overtype mode. Type

    D:\UTILITY

over the letters C:\PCPLUS. Our finished FAKEEXEC.BAT file looks like this:

```
C:\DOS\SMARTDRV.EXE
PROMPT $P$G
PATH=C:\DOS
SET PCPLUS=D:\UTILITY
SET TEMP=C:\TEMP
```

Good Idea #102: Saving All Your Hard Work

After making changes to your file, you must save it before exiting the editor (otherwise, you'll lose all changes to the file). If you don't want to save any changes at all, skip to the next section. To save your changes:

1. Open the File menu by clicking on it (press the left mouse button while the pointer is on the word File) or by pressing the **Alt** and **F** keys.

2. Select the **S**ave command by clicking on it or by pressing **S**.

3. If you want to keep your original file intact (without changes) and save this file under a new name, click on the Save As command, or press **A**. Type the new file name and press **Enter**.

Exiting the DOS 6 Editor

After you have saved your changes, you can safely exit the editor.

1. Open the File menu by clicking on it or by pressing the **Alt** and **F** keys.

2. Select the Exit command by clicking on it or by pressing X.

By the Way . . .

You can run your FAKEEXEC.BAT file by typing

```
CD\
FAKEEXEC
```

The commands in the FAKEEXEC.BAT are real DOS commands, just like the ones you might want in your actual AUTOEXEC.BAT. By running the FAKEEXEC batch file, you may have changed some system parameters that were set up by your real AUTOEXEC.BAT, so reboot your PC (press **Ctrl+Alt+Delete** at the same time) to reset your computer to the way it was. When you're done playing with it, delete the FAKEEXEC.BAT file so it won't cause any mix-ups by typing

DEL C:\FAKEEXEC.BAT

Meet Old Mr. EDLIN

If you don't have at least DOS 5, you get to use a simple—if a bit eccentric—editor called EDLIN to create and edit text files. But have no fear: there are only a few things you need to know in order to edit simple files, such as CONFIG.SYS and AUTOEXEC.BAT, and you can forget what you learn as soon as you're done.

One of the most common commands you add to your AUTOEXEC.BAT file is the PROMPT command. The PROMPT command changes the default DOS prompt from something boring like C>, to something fancy, like

C:\WORD\DOCS>

Let's add this command to our configuration file using EDLIN. Use FAKEEXEC.BAT if you're a beginner, and then modify AUTOEXEC.BAT later, after you've learned the procedure.

Get Started with EDLIN

Having created our FAKEEXEC.BAT file earlier, we can now experiment without having to worry. To start EDLIN in order to make changes to FAKEEXEC.BAT, type this:

EDLIN C:\FAKEEXEC.BAT

If you get the error message **Bad command or file name**, you need to set up a DOS path so that DOS can find the EDLIN command. For now, type this to start EDLIN:

CD\DOS
EDLIN C:\FAKEEXEC.BAT

Later, you can add a PATH command to your AUTOEXEC.BAT so that you can start EDLIN from any directory.

This command tells DOS to "Start the EDLIN program and open the file FAKEEXEC.BAT in the root directory of drive C." When you start EDLIN, the regular DOS prompt is replaced by an asterisk. You type commands at the asterisk to edit the file. Because you are editing an existing file, you will see this:

EDLIN C:\FAKEEXEC.BAT
End of input file
*

If you didn't do the FAKEEXEC.BAT project earlier, and you enter this command, DOS assumes you want to create the file. EDLIN displays the words, **New file**, followed by an asterisk. To begin working on a new file, you must start in Insert mode. Type the letter **I** and press **Enter** and you'll see this:

1:*

Turn back to the project to see what to type. When you've typed the three lines, press **Ctrl** and **C** at the same time. You've now left Insert mode and returned to Edit mode. Read more about Insert mode in the sections "Inserting New Lines" and "Getting Out of Insert Mode."

When It's Time for a Change

Let's go back to editing the FAKEEXEC.BAT file. After the file is loaded, start by listing the file's contents. Type this:

L

and press **Enter**. EDLIN shows a line-by-line listing of the file's contents.

```
C:\>EDLIN FAKEEXEC.BAT
End of input file
*L
        1:*C:\DOS\SMARTDRV.EXE
        2:  SET PCPLUS=C:\PCPLUS
        3:  SET TEMP=C:\TEMP
*
```

EDLIN lists a file's contents line by line.

With EDLIN, you edit files line by line, which is where EDLIN gets its name, "**Ed**it by **lin**e." Each line is assigned a number. This number becomes important, as we'll soon see.

Changing Your ~~Mind~~ Lines

Let's say you've re-installed the ProComm Plus program into a new directory called D:\UTILITY. You need to change the SET command on line 2 to reflect this. At the prompt (the asterisk), type

> 2

and press **Enter**. Line 2 appears, ready to edit:

> 2:*SET PCPLUS=C:\PCPLUS
> 2:*

EDLIN is waiting for you to type in the new line. Type this after the asterisk:

> **SET PCPLUS=D:\UTILITY**

and press **Enter**. Now, list the contents of the file so you can see what's happening. Type

> L

Because the first part of our line was a repeat of the existing text (SET PCPLUS=), you could have pressed the right arrow key 11 times (or just held it down) to make EDLIN type the first 11 characters of the line for you.

and press **Enter**, and you'll see this:

> **1: C:\DOS\SMARTDRV.EXE**
> **2:*SET PCPLUS=D:\UTILITY**
> **3: SET TEMP=C:\TEMP**

Inserting New Lines

Now, let's add a couple of lines to the FAKEEXEC.BAT, at the top of the file. To insert a line, type the number that you want the new line to be, followed by the letter I. (The existing line with that number moves down.) We want to insert some commands above the SET PCPLUS=C:\UTILITY line, which is line 2. Type this:

> **2I**

You'll see this:

> **2:***

Now, type these three commands after the asterisk, pressing **Enter** after each one:

> **PROMPT PG**
> **PATH=C:\DOS**
> **BOGUS COMMAND**

The first command changes your prompt so that it displays the current drive and directory. The second command provides access to certain DOS commands like EDIT. The last command is totally fake and it's there so you can practice deleting it. Authors are so clever, aren't they? After typing these commands, press **Enter**, and you'll see this:

> **2:*PROMPT PG**
> **3:*PATH=C:\DOS**
> **4:*BOGUS COMMAND**
> **5:***

Getting Out of Insert Mode

> ### By the Way . . .
> Insert mode is different in EDLIN than in EDIT. In EDIT, Insert mode means the existing characters move over to make room for what you type. Because EDLIN is line-based, Insert mode means whole lines move down to make room for new lines you enter.

When you're done inserting lines, you must turn off Insert mode. With your cursor on line 5 (a blank line), press the **Ctrl** and **C** keys at the same time. You'll be returned to the asterisk prompt. You are now out of Insert mode. Let's list the contents of our file. Type

L

and you'll see:

1: C:\DOS\SMARTDRV.EXE
2: PROMPT PG
3: PATH=C:\DOS
4: BOGUS COMMAND
5:*SET PCPLUS=D:\UTILITY
6: SET TEMP=C:\TEMP

> Always re-list the file after you have added or deleted lines. Line numbers shift when you add or delete, so the previous listing isn't accurate anymore, even though you may still see it on your screen.

Deleting a Line

Let's delete the BOGUS COMMAND line. When we listed out our file, the BOGUS COMMAND was line 4. To delete a line, type the number of the line to delete, followed by the letter D. Type this:

4D

As soon as you delete a line of text, you should list out your file, because the remaining lines get renumbered. Type

L

and you'll see:

```
1: C:\DOS\SMARTDRV.EXE
2: PROMPT $P$G
3: PATH=C:\DOS
4:*SET PCPLUS=D:\UTILITY
5: SET TEMP=C:\TEMP
```

Saving Your File

When you're finished editing, you can save and exit both in one step.
Type

E

The letter E means End, which saves your file and exits you from EDLIN.
You are returned to the DOS prompt.

By the Way . . .

You can run your FAKEEXEC.BAT file by typing

CD
FAKEEXEC

The commands in the FAKEEXEC.BAT are real DOS commands, just like the ones you might want in your actual AUTOEXEC.BAT. By running the FAKEEXEC batch file, you may have changed some system parameters that were set up by your real AUTOEXEC.BAT, so reboot your PC (press **Ctrl+Alt+Delete** all at the same time) to reset your computer to the way it was. When you're done playing with it, delete the FAKEEXEC.BAT file so it won't cause any mix-ups by typing

DEL C:\FAKEEXEC.BAT

Not Saving Your File

Sometimes, you make some mistakes in a file (especially with deleting), and you want to abort your changes and just get out of there. Type this:

Q

The letter Q means **Quit**. When you quit a file, you see the message, **Abort edit (Y/N)?**. Type **Y**, and your changes are abandoned (everything since starting EDLIN). Exit EDLIN and return to the DOS prompt.

The Least You Need to Know

Editing my configuration files used to give me chills until I learned these things:

- ☞ To create short files (if you're a good typist), type **COPY CON:** followed by the name of the file to create. When you are done, press **Enter** so you are on a blank line, then press **F6** and **Enter** at the same time. The file is saved.

- ☞ You should save your configuration files to your existing emergency diskette before editing them. Type

    COPY C:\AUTOEXEC.BAT A:
    COPY C:\CONFIG.SYS A:

- ☞ Reboot your computer to make the changes to your configuration files take effect.

- ☞ If you have at least DOS 5, you can edit files with EDIT. To start EDIT, type EDIT followed by the name of a file.

- ☞ To move around in EDIT, use the arrow keys. To insert a new line at the cursor, press **Enter**. To type over characters instead of inserting, press the **Insert** key. To return to Insert mode, press **Insert** again. To delete characters, use the **Delete** key.

continues

continued

☞ To save a file, press **Alt** and **F** to open the **File** menu. Press **S** to save the file.

☞ To exit EDIT, press **Alt** and **F** to open the **File** menu. Press **X** to exit.

☞ If you don't have at least DOS 5, use EDLIN to edit a file. To start EDLIN, type **EDLIN** followed by the name of a file.

☞ To list a file's contents in EDLIN, type **L**.

☞ To edit an existing line in EDLIN, type the line number.

☞ To insert lines, type the number of the line you want to follow your inserted lines followed by the letter I. For example, if you want to insert something in front of line 4, type **4I**.

☞ To exit Insert mode and resume regular editing, press **Enter** so you are on a blank line, then press **Ctrl** and **C** at the same time.

☞ To delete a line, use the list command first by typing **L**. Then delete a line by typing its number followed by **D**, as in **5D**.

☞ To save a file and exit EDLIN, type **E**.

☞ To abandon a file and not save the changes in EDLIN, type **Q**. When you see the message **Abort (Y/N)?**, press **Y**.

Chapter 17
Virus Got You Down?

In This Chapter

- ☛ What is a computer virus?
- ☛ How does a PC get a virus?
- ☛ How to get rid of a virus if your PC contracts one
- ☛ How to use the new DOS 6 anti-virus protection program
- ☛ Shopping for an anti-virus program

This chapter is all about bad things that go bump in the night. Before your computer starts acting like crazy Uncle Leroy, you owe it to yourself to read this chapter. The information in this chapter won't do much to help Uncle Leroy, but it may save your computer and, more importantly, your data from self-destruction.

Lions, Tigers, and Viruses, Oh My!

A *virus* is a program that infects your computer in various ways, such as changing your files, damaging your disks, and preventing your computer from starting.

You can infect your system anytime you copy or download files onto your hard disk or if you boot (start your system) with a diskette in drive A. You see, if a file has been infected by a virus and it gets on your system, that virus can spread. For example, if a virus has infected one of your programs, when you start that program, the virus may go into action.

Taking Your Vitamins
(and Other Ways to Protect Your PC)

You can protect your PC from serious damage by

☞ Maintaining a recent backup of your files (a process that copies files onto diskette or backup tape in a special format). By backing up important files onto a diskette or a tape, you can restore those files if the originals get damaged due to some virus (see Chapter 15 for more information).

☞ Checking diskettes for viruses before copying files from them. *Be sure to check program disks before installing new software.*

> ### By the Way . . .
>
> I know, I know . . . but unfortunately, you can't afford to trust anyone these days. Even if your new software came in shrink-wrapped packages, it could have been infected at the software company (there have been several reported cases of this happening). So don't take any chances. Check all disks for viruses before using them.

☞ Write-protecting program (installation) diskettes to prevent infection.

☞ Running a virus detection program (that works in the background) all the time.

☞ Never starting your computer with a diskette in the drive. (Make a virus-free bootable diskette for emergency purposes—see the next section.)

☞ Running a virus removal program as soon as a problem occurs.

Performing the Heimlich

If you haven't already, you need to create an emergency diskette now, before your system suffers from infection. You can create a virus-safe emergency diskette (as described in Chapter 13) by typing these commands:

> FORMAT A: /S /V
> COPY C:\CONFIG.SYS A:
> COPY C:\AUTOEXEC.BAT A:

If you have DOS 6, you should also copy the Microsoft Anti-Virus program onto the emergency diskette. Use these commands:

> COPY C:\DOS\MSAV.* A:

If you don't have DOS 6, read the next section, "What to Do If You Don't Have DOS 6—Other Virus Protection Programs."

Whether you have DOS 6 or you purchase some other virus protection software, keep in mind that new viruses are invented every day. Keep your virus detection current by updating the list of viruses. See your program manual for more details.

Keep your system files current by copying your CONFIG.SYS and AUTOEXEC.BAT files onto your emergency diskette whenever you modify them. After you've copied these files onto the diskette, write-protect it to prevent infection. If you ever need the diskette, you'll have a good copy of your system files and the virus detection program.

What to Do If You Don't Have DOS 6— Other Virus Protection Programs

Frankly, there are many reasons to upgrade to DOS 6, and the virus protection that's included with it is one mighty good reason. But if you're stuck with the DOS version you currently have, don't lose hope—there are many alternatives available:

By the Way . . .

If you use DOS and Windows like I do, make sure you buy an anti-virus program that can run both from within Windows and from the DOS prompt. The Microsoft Anti-Virus program that comes with DOS 6 is such a program, and most anti-virus programs you buy today offer this feature.

Central Point Anti-Virus This comes with the latest version of PC Tools, another Central Point product. The anti-virus program that comes with DOS 6 is a licensed version of this program.

Norton AntiVirus Another sure winner—very dependable. I use this one myself.

McAffee Virus Protection Tools This is an excellent shareware product (translation: it costs very little to buy, yet offers the same protection as the big guys).

Once you've acquired a good anti-virus program, copy it onto your emergency diskette as shown in the preceding section.

Starve a Cold, Feed a Fever: Things to Do Once a Virus Is Suspected

If you think that your computer is acting strange, don't assume that it's a computer virus. You may be using a program that's not installed properly, or your equipment may be going out. I've had weird things happen just because a cable was loose, so don't yell "The sky is falling!" until you're sure it is.

How do you know when you should panic? Well, if you own a good virus protection program, you can test your system for viruses before you call out the National Guard. When you suspect a problem:

1. Stop whatever you're doing. Return all tray tables and seat backs to their upright and locked positions, then exit all programs, including the DOS Shell or anything else you're running.

2. Reboot your PC with your emergency diskette. Now you'll find out why you created that thing in the first place. Put the emergency diskette in drive A and reboot by pressing the **Ctrl+Alt+Delete** keys at the same time.

3. Use your anti-virus program to scan for viruses. If a virus is detected, ask for it to be removed.

4. If you lose files, restore them from your backup. Before backing up files, you should check for viruses on your system. Then if you need to use the backup to replace files that were infected after the

backup was taken, you'll have virus-free files to restore. If you're not sure, run your virus detection program after restoring the damaged files.

If you have DOS 6, read the following section for detailed instructions on how to detect and remove viruses from your system.

Now This Won't Hurt a Bit: Scanning for Viruses with DOS 6

If you have DOS 6, you can use its virus detection program to scan for viruses. After exiting all programs and rebooting with your emergency diskette (see the last section), follow these steps to scan your disk:

1. Start the Microsoft Anti-Virus program. Type this:

   MSAV /A /C

   The /A switch tells Microsoft Anti-Virus to scan all drives but A and B, and the / C switch tells it to remove the viruses it finds. The scan won't take too long—about 15 minutes or so, depending on the size of your hard disk. If you are connected to a network, type this instead (this limits scanning to local drives only):

   MSAV /L /C

   You can stop the scan process at any time by pressing **F3**.

2. When it's over, go home. The Microsoft Anti-Virus program scans all your drives and cleans them of any viruses found. After the scan is complete, press **F3** to exit.

You'll Love Starting Up in the Morning

To perform a scan of your hard disk every time you boot your computer, add the following command to your AUTOEXEC.BAT file (hey, didn't we learn how to edit our AUTOEXEC.BAT file in the last chapter? Good timing!):

MSAV /N

The /N switch tells Microsoft Anti-Virus to load itself into memory and start a scan for viruses. If you are attached to a network, use this command instead:

MSAV /N /L

With one of these commands in place, your hard disk will be scanned automatically at startup. If any viruses are detected, a dialog box appears, offering several options:

- ☞ Choose **Clean** to clean the virus from your system.

- ☞ Choose **Continue** to ignore the virus, but continue scanning. If you know that a file was changed legitimately, use this option.

- ☞ Choose **Stop** to stop the scanning process and go to the Anti-Virus Main Menu.

- ☞ Choose **Delete** to delete the infected file from your system. Use this option if the file has been destroyed by a virus and you want to prevent further infection.

Round-the-Clock Protection with DOS 6

Using the MSAV command at startup will detect only viruses that are active at that time. To have ongoing protection, run VSafe. VSafe is a program that runs in the background as you perform your normal computer tasks. VSafe will warn you of changes to your files that might be caused by viruses. To start VSafe automatically every time you boot your computer, add this command to your AUTOEXEC.BAT:

VSAFE

The Least You Need to Know

I hate to get sick. I need to do a zillion things, but I'm too sick to do them. It's even more frustrating working with a sick computer, but you'll soon nurse it back to health if you remember these things:

☛ Don't panic if you suspect a virus—it could just be that soda you spilled on your keyboard last week.

☛ There are things you need to do now, before your PC gets a virus, like:

Creating an emergency diskette, and keeping it updated.

Always doing backups.

Checking diskettes for viruses before you use them—especially installation diskettes.

Write-protecting important diskettes so they don't contract a virus somewhere in the future.

Never leaving a diskette in its drive.

Running a virus detection program all the time.

Running a virus removal program as soon as you suspect trouble.

☛ To create an emergency diskette, use these commands:

FORMAT A: /S /V
COPY C:\CONFIG.SYS A:
COPY C:\AUTOEXEC.BAT A:

If you have a virus detection program, copy it onto the emergency diskette, too.

☛ To run the DOS 6 virus detection program, type **MSAV /A /C**. If you are attached to a network, use this command instead: **MSAV /L /C**.

continues

continued

☞ To scan your hard disk with the DOS 6 virus
protection program when you boot your PC, add
this command to your AUTOEXEC.BAT: **MSAV
/N**. If you are attached to a network, use this
command instead: **MSAV /N /L**.

☞ To continuously scan with the DOS 6 virus
detection program for viruses as you work, put
this command in your AUTOEXEC.BAT: **VSAFE**.

Chapter 18
Double Your Pleasure, Double Your Fun

In This Chapter

- ☛ What is disk compression?
- ☛ Popular programs you can use to compress your hard disk
- ☛ Using DOS 6's DoubleSpace to compress a drive
- ☛ Compressing a diskette with DoubleSpace

Is It Getting Crowded in Here?

Disk compression programs store more information on a disk because they use a kind of "computer shorthand" that allows them to store data in less space than with DOS alone. If you use a disk compression program, your hard disk can increase its storage capacity by almost two times.

Disk compression is not new; actually, the technology has been around for quite some time. The backup and restore programs that come with DOS use a compression technique similar to the kind used in disk compression programs. You can use a compressed drive the same way you would use any regular drive; the only difference is that the compressed drive will store more files than your hard disk normally would. One concern you may have is, "Will disk compression make my computer any slower than it already is?" Well, maybe a little, but we're talking computer time here (where things happen in the blink of an eye).

TECHNO NERD TEACHES

After you've installed a disk compression program, a huge file will eat most of your C drive. This huge file contains a compressed version of all of your files—think of that file as a trash-compacted version of your C drive.

Here's the tricky part. The disk compression program knows that you expect all the files that were on C: before to be accessible from C: now. But after disk compression, drive C is almost empty except for this huge file. So the disk compression program tells DOS to re-assign the drive letter C: to the *compressed* file and to change the name of the *real* C: to something else (like H: or I:). That way you can still do everything from the C: prompt as you did before you compressed your hard disk.

Popular Disk Compression Programs

If you have DOS 6, you're in luck; DOS 6 comes with its own disk compression program called DoubleSpace. If you don't have DOS 6, you can upgrade or purchase a disk compression program such as Stacker, by Stac Electronics.

Using DoubleSpace to Compress a Drive

Okay, DOS 6 users, it's time to compress. It takes roughly one minute per megabyte of data to compress your hard disk, so you might want to start the DoubleSpace setup program at the end of the day and run it overnight. To set up DoubleSpace, follow these steps:

1. Exit all programs, including the DOS Shell.

2. Change to the DOS directory by typing

   CD\DOS

3. Start the DoubleSpace setup program by typing

   DBLSPACE

4. Choose **Express** setup. If you want to compress a drive other than C: or to create an empty compressed drive, you'll need to use **Custom** setup. Grab some Oreos and get a guru to help you.

5. A small section of your drive will remain uncompressed. If you want to change the default letter for the uncompressed drive, do so before pressing **Enter**.

6. A message will appear that tells you how long the compression process will take. This is a one-time process that takes about one minute per megabyte. Press **C** to Continue (which will complete the compression process) or **Esc** to exit (which will stop it).

7. After the disk compression is finished, a summary will display, showing information on the compressed drive. Press **Enter** and your system will restart with the compressed drive active.

Once you compress a drive using DoubleSpace, you can shrink its size, but you can't reverse the compression process. As a safety precaution, do a full backup before running DoubleSpace (see Chapter 14).

If you want to display information about your compressed drive, type this:

DIR /C

If you depend on third-party utilities such as disk optimizers, disk repair utilities, memory managers, and anti-virus programs, make sure that they are compatible with your disk compression software. If you're not sure, consult the manual or call the manufacturer before you run these programs.

Now That I Have a Compressed Drive, What Do I Do with It?

You work with your compressed drive as you would with any other drive. The compression process remains invisible to you, the user. The DoubleSpace maintenance program allows you to perform the compression functions listed here. You access the DoubleSpace maintenance program by typing

DBLSPACE

From the DoubleSpace maintenance program, you can

- ☛ Increase the storage capacity of diskettes by compressing them.
- ☛ Adjust the size of your compressed drive.
- ☛ Display information about the compressed drive.
- ☛ Format a compressed drive.
- ☛ *Defragment* a compressed drive.
- ☛ Check a compressed drive for lost clusters and chains with a variation of the CHKDSK command.

Defragmentation When you modify a file, the changes often get written to a different spot on the disk than the original file. Files with pieces in more than one place are called *fragmented*. A defragmenting program rewrites data on the disk so that all the pieces of a file are in the same physical spot. Defragmenting can improve disk performance and efficiency.

Compressing a Diskette with DoubleSpace

Once you've installed DoubleSpace on your hard disk, you can use it for diskettes to improve their storage capacities. After a diskette has been compressed by DoubleSpace, it will hold almost twice as much data as before. I don't want to throw you into a compression depression, but there is one drawback to using compressed diskettes: you can use a compressed diskette only on a PC that uses DOS 6, and is running DoubleSpace.

To compress a diskette, insert the diskette in its drive, then type this:

DBLSPACE

Then compress the diskette by following these steps:

1. Open the Compress menu. Click on the menu (press the left mouse button while pointing to the word Compress) or press the **Alt** and **C** keys at the same time.

2. Select the Existing Drive command. Click on the command with the mouse or use the down arrow key to highlight it, then press **Enter**.

3. If necessary, change the drive to compress. Use the arrow keys to select a drive to compress, and press **Enter**. Press **C** to continue.

4. After the disk is compressed, return to DOS. Open the **Drive** menu and select the Exit command by clicking on them with the mouse. If you're using the keyboard, press the **Alt** and **D** keys at the same time, then press the letter **X**.

Now that the diskette has been compressed, use the diskette as you would any other. But while you are using it, do not remove it from its drive or reboot, or you'll have to mount it to use it again. Mounting is the process that DoubleSpace goes through in order to make the compressed files available to DOS.

If you need to mount a compressed diskette in order to use it, insert the diskette into its drive, then type

DBLSPACE MOUNT A:

If you need to mount a compressed diskette in drive B, type

DBLSPACE MOUNT B:

The Least You Need to Know

I never thought I'd find enough stuff to fill my new 120MB hard disk, but it was almost filled in a week. Until I used DoubleSpace, I thought I'd have to invest in another computer. Now I've got plenty of room (at least 'til the end of the month). When using a disk compression program, remember these things:

☞ Disk compression programs store more information on a disk using a special "computer shorthand."

☞ Popular disk compression programs include DOS 6's DoubleSpace and Stac Electronic's Stacker.

☞ To install DoubleSpace, change to the DOS directory, and then type **DBLSPACE.**

   Choose **Express** setup, then type the drive to compress, and press **Enter**. Press **C** to continue, and the compression begins.

☞ To display information about a compressed drive, type **DIR /C.**

continues

continued

☞ To compress a diskette with DoubleSpace, type **DBLSPACE**.

Open the **C**ompress menu by pressing the **Alt** and **C** keys at the same time. Press **X** to select the Existing Drive command. When the disk is compressed, press the **Alt** and **D** keys at the same time to open the **D**rive menu. Press **X** to select Exit.

☞ A compressed disk must be mounted in order to use it. After a disk is compressed by DoubleSpace, it is automatically mounted. However, if you remove the diskette or reboot, it must be remounted in order to use it. To mount a diskette, place it in its drive, then type **DBLSPACE MOUNT A:** or **DBLSPACE MOUNT B:**.

Chapter 19
Did I Forget to Tell You About Computer Memory?

In This Chapter

- ☛ What is memory, and why should you care about it?

- ☛ Displaying the amount of available memory

- ☛ Simple things you can do to improve your computer's memory

- ☛ Using MemMaker to automatically improve your computer's use of memory

So What Is Memory?

Random-access memory, or *RAM*, is the working area of your computer, like a desktop. The amount of RAM you have determines how much "desk" space DOS has to work with.

Let's say you have a drawer full of client folders at work. To work with a folder, you retrieve it from the drawer and put it on your desktop. In the same way, when you start a program, the program files are loaded into RAM from a disk. As you use the program to create documents, those documents take up space in RAM, too. If you run complex programs or create large documents, you need lots of RAM.

And Why Should I Care?

All programs need memory to run—some
need quite a lot of memory. Not having
enough memory can affect the way your
programs work and can even prevent some
programs from starting.

   Although your computer may have lots of
RAM, the portion of it that DOS can use
directly is very limited, as you'll learn later in
this chapter. That's why it's important to
make the most of each bit. By managing this
precious resource effectively, you can

> **Have a faster, more efficient PC.**   How many of us plan our coffee
> breaks around when we use certain programs because we know they
> take so long to retrieve a file, perform calculations, or sort data?

> **Resolve "out of memory" problems.**   Everything that your computer
> needs to use must go into memory: programs, data files, and even DOS.
> It's easy to see how this precious resource can get used up pretty quickly.
> Nothing is more frustrating than a program that won't start or acts
> funny because your computer doesn't have room for all its "stuff."

> **Exploit memory usage to the fullest**.   I recently visited my boyfriend's
> parents for Christmas, and we had to fit suitcases, Christmas presents,
> and half-finished Christmas projects into a trunk the size of a bread box.
> Your computer's memory is like the trunk of a car. By helping your
> computer manage its memory better, you'll be amazed at what can fit
> into memory: a pop-up day planner, an anti-virus program, the DOS
> Shell, your word processor, and maybe even a spreadsheet program.

Tell Me More About Memory

RAM is divided into several sections. The area of RAM that DOS uses
directly, as the main desktop, is called *conventional memory*. Conventional
memory is the first 640 kilobytes of RAM in your computer's memory
banks. The rest of RAM is useful only for system files, or for temporary data
storage.

The abbreviations K and MB in the figure stand for kilobyte and megabyte, two measures of RAM. You'll learn more about them in the next section.

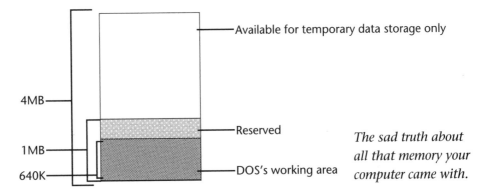

4MB

1MB

640K

Available for temporary data storage only

Reserved

DOS's working area

The sad truth about all that memory your computer came with.

How Much Memory Does Your Computer Have?

Computers can understand only two things: 1 or 0. (This makes computers smarter than children who understand only one thing: the word "Yes"—and not the word "No.") Each 1 or 0 is a *bit*, or binary di**git**. Place eight bits in a row, and you have a *byte*, which can represent any single character (such as the number 2 or the letter J).

A *kilobyte* (1K) is roughly a thousand bytes (1,024 bytes, to be exact). A *megabyte* (1MB) is roughly a million bytes (1,048,576 bytes).

Most computers today come with at least 2MB to 4MB of RAM, broken down like this: 640K of conventional memory, 360K of upper memory, and the rest in extended memory. As you learned earlier in the chapter, only the first 640K can be used to run programs. Now, here comes an even bigger kick in the pants: part of that miserly 640K chunk of memory is used by DOS for itself. To check this out, exit all programs, then type this command:

CHKDSK

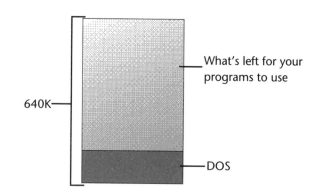

You mean I don't even have 640K to run all my programs in?

If you look at the bottom set of numbers in the listing, you'll see the horrible truth: of the total 655,360 bytes (640K), you have maybe 510,512 bytes left.

Since you're not running any programs, what's taking up part of memory? The answer is DOS. DOS itself is loaded into memory. DOS needs a place to work (to interpret your commands and control information flow), so it grabs a piece of conventional memory for itself.

Using the MEM Command to See the Whole Picture

CHKDSK only displays information about the first 640K of memory. If you have at least DOS 5, you can use this command to see all about memory:

MEM

MEM will tell you how much conventional, upper, and extended memory you have as well as how much is available at the moment. MEM will also display expanded memory information if you have an expanded memory circuit board or if you've converted any of your extended memory into expanded memory.

By the Way . . .

There are four types of memory. The first 640K of RAM is *conventional memory*, and it is the only place where programs can run and where DOS can manipulate data. From 640K to 1MB is a wasteland called *upper memory*. Upper memory is reserved for DOS, and the programs for handling input (data coming into the computer) and output (data going out of the computer) are stored there.

If you have at least DOS 5, part of upper memory can be reclaimed for storing *device drivers* (special programs that help DOS use optional devices, such as a mouse) and *TSRs* (pop-up programs that run in the background, such as a calculator you can "pop up" while in your word processor or some other program). This can often free up a small amount of conventional memory.

After 1MB, the rest of RAM is called *extended memory*. (This is that temporary data storage area we were just talking about.) Programs that are written to recognize this storage area can speed up their operations by stashing temporary files there rather than writing them to a disk.

Expanded memory is extra memory that sometimes comes on a special circuit board, but it is more often converted from extended memory. Expanded memory serves the same purpose as extended—it just goes about its business differently. Some programs can use either extended or expanded memory, but most programs want one or the other.

Simple Things That Improve Memory Usage

If you have DOS 5, you can add these commands to the *beginning* of your CONFIG.SYS file:

```
DEVICE=C:\DOS\HIMEM.SYS
DOS=HIGH
```

These two commands move DOS (or most of it anyway) out of conventional memory, into a nonconventional part of RAM that normally goes unused. This gives your programs more room in conventional memory to run.

If you have a PC that has a 386 CPU, you can do some other things to really improve the memory management of your PC. Accessing the other areas of memory can be kind of tricky, so ask a PC guru to help you.

DOS 6 Users: Just Sit Back and Relax

If you have DOS 6, you can thank your lucky stars. DOS 6 comes with a memory manager called MemMaker that is a dream to use. MemMaker is designed to automatically make changes that will allow you to optimize your system's memory.

By the Way . . .

MemMaker is great, but it's not perfect. A PC guru who knows all the tricks can optimize your system's memory usage better than MemMaker can. If you want to know more about memory and how to make the most of it, read *10 Minute Guide to Memory Management*. (Watch out: this is a blatant plug for another book I've written.)

MemMaker is very easy to use, and it provides fairly good results. To optimize your system with MemMaker, exit all programs, then type this command:

MEMMAKER

Press **Enter** and a message appears, asking you to choose between Express (for real people like us) and Custom optimization (for confident users—like geeks). To use Express, press **Enter**. To switch to Custom, press the **Spacebar**, then **Enter**. Let's assume you chose the easy way out—Express installation. Follow these steps:

1. A message appears, asking if you use any programs that require expanded memory. If a program requires this type of memory, it should say so on the box it came in. If you're not sure, pick **No**. You can always change it later.

2. A message appears, asking you to press Enter. Do it, and MemMaker will restart your computer.

3. MemMaker makes changes to your AUTOEXEC.BAT and CONFIG.SYS (your old files are saved with a .UMB extension). Press **Enter**, and MemMaker will test your new configuration.

4. A message appears, asking if your new configuration is OK. Press **Enter** for Yes if the computer restarted okay, or press the **Spacebar** and then **Enter** to answer No and continue testing.

5. A listing showing your system's memory usage appears. Press **Enter** to exit MemMaker.

The Least You Need to Know

I better tell you this stuff about memory before I forget:

- ☛ RAM is the working area of the computer where information is processed.

- ☛ Conventional memory is the first 640K of RAM. Conventional memory is the most important part of RAM because it is the only part where a program can run and where data can be manipulated.

- ☛ Memory is divided into bytes. A byte stores a single character, such as the letter Q. A *kilobyte* (1K) is roughly a thousand bytes, and a *megabyte* (1MB) is roughly a million bytes.

- ☛ If you have at least DOS 5, you can use the MEM command to display memory usage.

continues

continued

☞ If you have at least DOS 5, you can add these commands to the beginning of your CONFIG.SYS file, and free up some of the conventional memory your PC uses:

DEVICE=C:\DOS\HIMEM.SYS
DOS=HIGH

☞ If you have DOS 6, you can use MemMaker to configure the memory in your system. Type **MEMMAKER** to start MemMaker.

Part Four
Back in the Real World

Someone somewhere decided that you needed a computer to get your work done faster and more efficiently. That person may even have provided some basic programs for you to use. Now you're sitting there thinking, "Great. They tell me this thing is going to save me a lot of time and trouble, and I just spent a half hour trying to turn it on!" This section deals with the trials and tribulations of learning to install, start, and use new programs—with or without the "help" of manuals.

Chapter 20
A Simple Guide to Software

In This Chapter

☛ How to get help when you need it

☛ A guide to the types of programs available

☛ How to install a program like a pro

☛ How to start a program when no one's shown you how

☛ How to navigate the most popular menu systems

☛ Easy ways to select commands and get work done

☛ A special look at the Lotus 1-2-3 menu system

☛ How to navigate dialog boxes and select commands in them

The one thing that most beginners don't realize is how little they really need to know. Once you've learned the basics in one program, you can wing your way through the next one because most programs today follow the same basic format.

Think of buying a new car: no manufacturer would design a car so that the ignition key is inserted on the left side of the steering column, instead of the right side. This move to "be different" would be met with disbelief and dismal sales. Why? Because no one enjoys having to "learn things all over again." So, like car manufacturers, programmers for the most part design their programs to follow the same set of rules as everyone else. The benefit to you is obvious: once you've learned how to use one program, you'll spend less than half that time learning the next, and so on.

Get Your Programs Here!

A computer is no better than a boat anchor unless it has a *program* to tell it what to do. A program is a set of instructions written in special "machine language" that the computer understands. A program tells the computer to perform some particular task, such as acting like a typewriter or a calculator. Other programs tell your computer to act like a drawing pad, a stereo, a day planner, and many other things.

One standard that most programs follow is how to access help. In almost every program I can name, you press F1 to get help. If you remember nothing else from this lesson, remember that. Of course, there is no guarantee that a programmer will follow this standard—after all, it's not law, but maybe it should be. So I have no explanation why WordPerfect insists that F3 is the help key.

There are many types of computer programs you can buy:

A program that tells the computer to act like a typewriter is called a word processor. To write a report or a family newsletter, use a word processor, such as Microsoft Word, WordPerfect, or Ami Pro. If you want to balance a checkbook or last year's budget, use a spreadsheet program. Some popular spreadsheet programs are Lotus 1-2-3 and Excel.

A program that organizes (and reorganizes) information in different ways is called a database manager. If you want to create an address book, or a customer list, or even a recipe file, use a database manager, such as dBASE IV, Q&A, FoxPro, or Microsoft Access. To create your own pictures for reports, presentations, or just for fun, use a painting and drawing program, such as PC Paintbrush, Corel Draw!, or Windows Draw!.

Desktop Publishing programs let you combine text and graphics into a finished page. This book was assembled in a desktop publishing program. Simple desktop publishing programs can create banners, signs, and calendars. More complex programs can create anything that combines text and pictures, such as newsletters, brochures, and reports. Popular desktop publishing programs include Publish It!, Express Publisher, First Publisher, Newsroom, PageMaker, and Ventura Publisher.

Utility programs are actually several small programs sold together that perform you-never-know-when-you'll-need-it tasks like undeleting files and recovering from system problems. Don't leave home without one of these. Popular utility programs include PC Tools, Norton Utilities, and Mace Utilities.

Modem A modem converts computer data into beeping noises that can be transmitted through an ordinary telephone line. At the receiving end, a modem converts the beeping noises back into computer data.

A program that helps your computer talk to another one through a *modem* is called a communications program. If you need to send data to other offices, or if you want to connect to an on-line information service, such as CompuServe or GEnie, you'll need a modem and this type of program. Some popular communications programs include ProComm Plus, Smartcom and Crosstalk. Some on-line services, such as Prodigy, use their own software.

If you are tired of starting your spreadsheet program by typing a series of mysterious commands, get yourself a menu program, and all you have to press is a number. Popular menu programs include Direct Access and Automenu. If you're looking for something fun, try a game program. Many popular games have been computerized—such as poker, backgammon, and chess. Action-adventure and flight simulators are also popular. (Don't use this type of program at work—unless you're the boss!)

Screen savers blank out your screen or replace it with pretty pictures whenever you leave your PC unattended for a few minutes. Programs like these prevent *burn-in*, which leaves a ghostly image of a program permanently etched into your PC's monitor. Popular screen savers include After Dark and Intermission.

With a DOS shell, you can perform all of the
same wonderful things you can with DOS, but
without the headache of remembering exactly
what to type. Shells get their name because they
protect you (like a shell) from DOS hassles. Don't
think that using a shell will make you a DOS
turtle—using a shell is easy, fast, and fun. Some
popular shells include the DOS Shell (which comes
with DOS versions 4 and higher), PC Shell (which
comes with PC Tools, a utility program), Norton
Commander, and Windows (which is much more
than a shell, and a whole lot of fun to use). If you
want to know more about using these types of programs with DOS, see
Chapter 21. For information on how to use the DOS Shell, see Chapter 7.

By the Way . . .

Don't worry that you won't be able to find the right program
for your needs. There are so many software programs on the
market these days that the right program is as easy to find as
a rerun of "It's a Wonderful Life" at Christmas. If anything,
you may be overwhelmed by the sheer number of choices.
Ask the clerks at the software store for their recommenda-
tions.

Installing Programs like a Pro

If you're a beginner, you may want to ask someone else to install programs
for you. But if you need it done now, you're the best person to do it, so
here goes:

1. Open the box, unwrap the diskettes, and check them for viruses.
    If you have DOS 6, type this command:

    MSAV A:

    If not, use a virus protection program such as Norton Anti-Virus
    or Central Point Anti-Virus.

2. Make copies of the diskettes. Making copies of installation diskettes will provide a backup should something happen to the originals. Before you copy, *write-protect* the disks. Then use DISKCOPY (see Chapter 13) to copy each diskette.

Write-protect When a disk is write-protected, it can be read, but not changed. On a 3 1/2-inch diskette, slide the tab up so the hole is exposed. On a 5 1/4-inch diskette, stick a black tab (included with the labels) over the side notch.

3. Find out some basic information about your PC before you try to install. The installation program may ask you things like what type of monitor you have and what type of printer. Look for names or other trademarks. If you have the owner's manual to your PC and its components, check there. If all else fails, ask a co-worker. Most companies buy in quantities, so you might have the same system as the person next to you.

4. Read the manual. I know, I know . . . but even I read the manual just to be sure before I try to install some strange new software. Look for an Installation Guide, or look for "Setup" or "Installation" in the user's manual.

5. If you've misplaced the manual or it's unclear, stick the first installation diskette in its drive and type something like this:

DIR A:*.EXE /P

Begin by looking for something like SETUP.EXE or INSTALL.EXE. If you find a SETUP.EXE file, type something like this to install the program:

A:
SETUP

If you don't find an appropriate .EXE file to install your program, try this command:

DIR A:*.BAT /P

If you see an error message that says that Windows needs to be running, you should start that program first, then install. Type

WIN

Once Windows is started, open the **File** menu in the Program Manager by clicking on it or by pressing the **Alt** and **F** keys at the same time. Select the **Run** command by clicking on it or by pressing **R**. Type the command to start the installation, as in

A:INSTALL

and press **Enter.**

Look for a file such as INSTALL.BAT or SETUP.BAT. If you can't find anything appropriate, the program may have been installed the old-fashioned way: by creating a directory and copying the files. Type something like this to install the program (change the directory name to one that you prefer):

MD C:\NEWPROGRM
COPY A:*.* C:\NEWPROGRM

6. *If you're given a choice, choose Express or Easy installation.* This type of installation will install your program with the least amount of fuss. Answer any questions that the installation program asks, and whenever possible, choose the defaults. You'll probably need to use the arrow keys to choose something from a list, and then press **Enter** to select it.

Starting Programs like a Pro

Now that you've installed your program, let's see how you might start it if there's no one around to help.

First, check the manual for the proper command. If you can't find it, go exploring:

DIR C:*. /P

This command lists all the main directories on your C drive (along with any files that don't have extensions; ignore these). Look for a directory with today's date. That's a new directory, so that's probably it. Type something like this:

CD\FASTACTG

This command will take you to \FASTACTG. Now look for a file to start the program:

DIR *.EXE /P

You're looking for something obvious. For example, if you just bought a program called Fast Accountant, you might see FA.EXE or FAST.EXE, or something similar. Type its name, and you'll probably start the program:

FAST

If you didn't find anything appropriate, try

DIR *.COM

OR

DIR *.BAT

Still not in the program? Go find a PC guru to help you.

Menu Mania

Once you make it inside the program, you may see some menus. Menus present lists of commands to choose from, so you don't have to memorize a lot of key combinations.

Menus are usually tucked away in a menu bar at the top of the screen. The menu bar lists the main menus, such as File, Edit, and Help. Under each of these menus, there are additional selections, but you can't see them until you *pull down* (open) the menu.

Pull down   A *pull-down* menu contains commands you can select. This type of menu, when activated, is pulled down below the main menu bar, as a window shade can be pulled down from the top of a window frame.

Menu System Conventions

Most menu systems make use of these conventions:

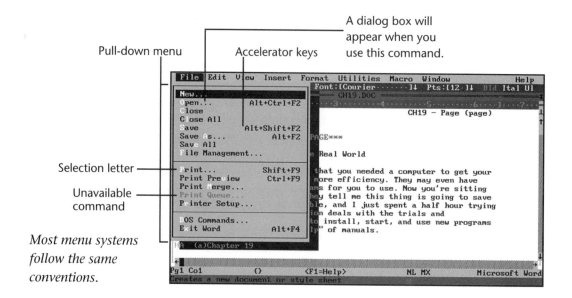

A dialog box will appear when you use this command.

Pull-down menu   Accelerator keys

Selection letter

Unavailable command

Most menu systems follow the same conventions.

Grayed text   Commands that are currently unavailable will be grayed to prevent you from selecting them.

Selection letter   A single letter of a menu command, such as *x* in Exit, that can be used to activate the command with the keyboard when the menu is open. Selection letters appear as underlined or bold letters on the main menu.

Accelerator keys   Like selection letters, these can be used to activate the command with the keyboard. Unlike selection letters, however, accelerator keys work without opening the menu. Usually a function key or key combination, such as Alt+F2, are displayed next to the menu command. To use an accelerator key, press the first key (in this case, **Alt**) and hold, then press the second key (in this, case **F2**).

Dialog box   A dialog box is a special window that appears when the program requires additional information before executing a command.

Ellipsis   An ellipsis consists of three periods after a menu command, such as the File Save As... command. An ellipsis indicates that after you've chosen this command, a *dialog box* appears, requiring you to provide more specific information before the command is executed.

Take Your Pick: Selecting Menu Commands

It's easy to select menu commands using either the mouse or the keyboard.

To select a menu command with the mouse, click (press the left mouse button) while pointing to the menu name. For example, click on the word File. While the menu is open, click once on the menu command to select it.

If there is an accelerator key for a command, you can press the key combination to activate the command, instead of opening the menu. For example, to select the **File S**ave command in the first figure in this chapter, you can press the **Alt**, **Shift**, and **F2** keys at the same time.

To select a menu command with the keyboard, press Alt plus the selection letter at the same time. For example, to open the File pull-down menu, press **Alt** and **F** at the same time. While the menu is open, use the arrow keys to highlight the command, and then press **Enter** to select it. Alternatively, you can press the selection letter for the command. For example, with the File menu open, you can select the Save command by pressing the letter **S**.

Talking to Your Computer with Dialog Boxes

When you select a menu command that requires additional information, a dialog box appears. Commands that result in the display of dialog boxes appear on menus with an ellipsis, as in the File Save As... command.

There are a few standard components of dialog boxes:

List box   Presents a list of items to choose from, such as a list of files.

Text box   Allows the user to type or edit information, such as the name of a file.

Drop-down list box   Like a normal list box, except that the list does not display until activated. The list displays under the main list item, like a window shade.

Check boxes   Check boxes are used to indicate options that can be turned on or off, such as Read Only.

Option buttons   Option buttons are used to select mutually exclusive options, such as Right, Center, or Left alignment.

Command buttons   Perform some specific command, such as OK or Cancel.

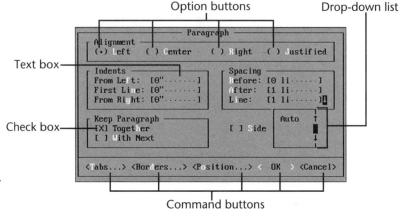

A typical dialog box.

Making the Right Choice

In some dialog boxes, you will be presented with many different components, such as list boxes and option buttons, where you need to make several choices. You can use either the mouse or the keyboard when making these choices in a dialog box.

To move around in a dialog box with the keyboard, move between dialog components by pressing **Tab** to move forward, and **Shift** and **Tab** to move backward. Alternatively, you can press **Alt** plus the highlighted letter of the dialog component. For example, to move in a dialog box to a list box named Directories, press **Alt** and **D**.

To make choices in a dialog box with the keyboard, use the arrow keys. In a list box, you may also use the Home, End, PgUp, and PgDn keys. To select an option button or check box, use the **Spacebar** to toggle the option on or off.

To move around a dialog box with the mouse, click (point to it and press the left mouse button) on any item. To select an option button or checkbox, click on it to toggle the option on or off.

You'll meet some of these standard command buttons while using dialog boxes: select **Cancel** to cancel the choices you have made in the dialog box and return to your program. Select the **Close** button to retain the choices you made and close the dialog box without executing those choices. If you want to close the dialog box and execute your choices, use the **OK** button.

A Special Look at the Lotus Menu System

Some programs use what is known as the Lotus menu system, made popular by the spreadsheet program Lotus 1-2-3. The Lotus menu bar appears at the top of the screen like most menu systems, but when a main menu is selected, the menu commands appear across the screen instead of on a pull-down menu.

File menu commands

Lotus uses a horizontal menu system that works differently from the standard pull-down menu.

Description of command

Although you can select Lotus commands with a mouse, most people don't. It's too easy to just use the keyboard. To select a menu command with the keyboard, press / to display the menu. Then use the left or right arrow keys to highlight a menu, and press **Enter**. Use the left or right arrow keys to select a command.

You can also select a menu or a command by pressing its first letter. For example, to select the File menu with the menu displayed, press **F**. To select the Save command on the File menu, press **S** with the File menu displayed. The entire sequence to select the File **S**ave command consists of three keystrokes: /, **F**, and **S**.

The Least You Need to Know

You won't need AAA to jumpstart your applications if you remember these basics:

☞ In most programs, you access help by pressing **F1**.

☞ You can use these commands to search for the file that starts the installation program:

DIR A:*.EXE /P

DIR A:*.BAT /P

DIR A:*.COM /P

You are looking for a file such as INSTALL.EXE or SETUP.EXE. When you find it, type something like **A:SETUP**.

☞ To select a command from a menu with the keyboard, press **Alt** plus the shortcut key at the same time. While the menu is open, use the arrow keys to highlight the command, and then press **Enter** to select it.

To select a menu command with the mouse, click (press the left mouse button) while pointing to the menu name.

☞ To select a command in a program that uses the Lotus menu system, press /, the first letter of the menu, and then the first letter of the command.

☞ Move between dialog box components by pressing **Tab** to move forward, and **Shift** and **Tab** to move backward. You can also press **Alt** plus the high-lighted letter of the dialog component.

☞ To make choices in a dialog box with the keyboard, use the arrow keys. In a list box, you may also use the Home, End, PgUp, and PgDn keys. To select an option button or check box, use the **Spacebar** to toggle the option on or off.

☞ To move around a dialog box with the mouse, click on any item. To select an option button or check-box, click on it to toggle the option on or off.

Chapter 21
Using DOS from Within Other Programs

In This Chapter

- ☛ What is a temporary command prompt?

- ☛ Commands you should not use while at a temporary prompt

- ☛ How do I get back to my regular program?

Some programs (Windows being a very famous example) allow you to sneak out to DOS to perform some command, then sneak back to the program, without having to exit the program at all. Why would you want to do this? Well, consider the following scenario:

Suppose you were working madly away in your spreadsheet program, and you decided to save an important document onto a diskette, but you weren't sure if there was enough room. Before you tried to save the file, you could use this command, if only you could get to a DOS prompt:

DIR A:

The DIR command would tell you what files were on the diskette and how much space was left. While you were at the DOS prompt, you could even delete some files from the diskette to make more room, as in

DEL A:OLD.DOC

Why, with access to DOS, you could even format a new diskette if necessary:

FORMAT A: /V

The possibilities are endless, but the problem is simple: you gotta get to DOS, but you don't want to quit your spreadsheet program just yet.

Well, if your application provides a temporary DOS prompt, you can get to DOS without actually exiting your program. Not all applications provide this service, but to learn how to use one, read on . . . .

Getting to DOS and Back

When you "exit" to the temporary DOS prompt, you're working in a protected environment that keeps your main application "safe" while you perform various DOS commands.

The command you use to access a temporary command prompt will vary by application (assuming the application even includes one). But it goes something like this:

1. From within the application, select the command to access the temporary prompt. Look for commands like "Command Prompt" or "DOS Commands" or "Shell" or some such.

> ## By the Way . . .
> I use both Windows and DOS like a lot of people, so I thought I'd take a moment to give you Windows users some specifics. If you want to use the temporary DOS prompt from within Windows, simply select the MS-DOS Prompt icon from within the Main program group.

2. Type your DOS command like usual. Nothing special—just type the command as you normally would. There are some commands you should avoid using; these are explained in the next section.

3. Return to your application when you are through. Regardless of what application you're using, there is one similarity in every temporary DOS prompt—and that's how to return to your application. Just type

   EXIT

What You Shouldn't Do While Using a Temporary DOS Prompt

Remember that even though you are typing commands at a temporary DOS prompt, your application is still running. You should take care not to use certain commands:

DEL Be sure you don't accidentally delete any important program files.

CHKDSK Don't use the /F parameter; it can change file information that your program may be using.

REN Don't rename any files your program may be using.

FORMAT Formatting a diskette is okay, but if you replace a diskette that the program was using with another one, make sure you put the original diskette back into its drive before you return to your application.

FASTOPEN, SHARE, APPEND, JOIN, and SUBST If you don't know what these commands are for, that's okay; just don't use them while in a shell.

DBLSPACE or some other disk compression utility Because these change the way files are stored, they could really mix up your application.

DEFRAG or any other disk optimizer Because these rearrange files on the hard disk, they'll make your application think it's on drugs. Don't use them while in a shell.

Any command that starts a program   Starting a program within another program may not be a great idea. Return from the temporary DOS prompt and exit your application before you start another program.

The Least You Need to Know

Before the age of temporary DOS prompts, working in an application was like trying to take a shower (that DOS phone was always ringing). You won't "slip on the soap" getting in and out of an application if you remember that:

- ☛ A temporary DOS prompt is a special part of an application (such as a word processor) that allows the user access to DOS without having to exit the main program.

- ☛ After using a temporary DOS prompt, type **EXIT** to return to your application.

- ☛ There are some commands you should be careful using while in a DOS shell: DEL, FORMAT, APPEND, CHKDSK, FASTOPEN, JOIN, REN, SHARE, SUBST, DBLSPACE, DEFRAG, and any command that starts another program.

Part Five
Problems That Lots of Us Have, and How to Fix Them

Contrary to popular opinion, computers are really very hard to break. Computers don't always understand exactly what you want them to do, so you might think that they're broken when they're really just being stupid. The information you'll find in these special sections will help you get over the rough spots when your computer refuses to understand.

Help! What Does This Message Mean, and What Should I Do?

There are few things more cryptic than DOS error messages (except maybe a Twin Peaks rerun, the meaning behind a Calvin Klein commercial, or my handwriting). Even veteran users can't always tell what DOS means when it issues an error—but don't worry—in this section, you'll find the cures for what ails you. Here you'll find a listing of the most common DOS error messages, complete with a list of what happened and what you should do now.

Access denied

What happened:

You tried to delete a file that's protected.

What you should do now:

You should probably not delete this file, because files are usually protected for a reason. If you feel that you need to delete this file, ask a PC guru for advice.

Bad command or file name

What happened (1):

You mistyped the command.

What you should do now:

Oops! Check the spelling of the command and any file name. Verify that you did not enter extra spaces where they are not needed.

What happened (2):

The command you tried to use is an external command, and DOS didn't recognize it.

What you should do now:

Type **PATH** and verify that **C:\DOS** is a part of the path. See Chapter 4 for more information on setting up a PATH for DOS to follow.

What happened (3):

You might have tried to start a program that lives in a directory DOS can't find. The directory might not exist anymore.

What you should do now:

Move to the program directory by typing something like this: **CD*PROGRAM*.** If you use this program a lot, you may want to add the program's directory to your DOS path. See Chapter 4 for more information on how to set up a PATH for DOS to follow.

Bad or missing command interpreter

What happened (1):

You've just exited a program that you started from a diskette.

What you should do now:

You should not remove a diskette that a program is using. Reboot the computer (press **Ctrl+Alt+Delete**), and it should be okay.

What happened (2):

The COMMAND.COM file that is normally in the root directory of your C drive has been accidentally deleted, or while copying all the files from a diskette, you've copied an older version of the COMMAND.COM file onto your drive.

What you should do now:

Reboot the computer (press **Ctrl+Alt+Delete**) with your emergency diskette in drive A, then type this: **COPY A:COMMAND.COM C:**.

Bad sectors

What happened:

After you've formatted a diskette, a number of bad sectors may be displayed. The diskette may be damaged, or you may have formatted the diskette to the wrong density.

What you should do now:

Verify that you formatted the diskette to the proper density.

Current drive is no longer valid

What happened:

You removed a diskette before a function was complete, or you were trying to use a diskette drive that didn't have a diskette in it.

What you should do now:

Put the diskette in the diskette drive. If you want to make drive A the current drive, type **A:** at the prompt. If you want to return to drive C, type **C:** at the prompt.

Data error reading drive *x*

What happened:

A file was damaged.

What you should do now:

Press **R** for Retry. If that doesn't work and the message returns, press **A** for Abort. Try to locate another copy of the file (say, on a backup) and use it instead. If the file is on a diskette, try reinserting the diskette in its drive. If you have any disk utilities, such as Norton Utilities, you might be able to repair a damaged diskette.

Duplicate file name or file not found

What happened:

You used the REN command to rename a file, but the new file name already exists.

What you should do now:

Try the command with another name, as in **REN OLDFILE.DOC NEWFILE.DOC.**

Errors found, F parameter not specified

What happened:

You used the CHKDSK command but did not include the /F switch. Errors on the hard disk were found.

What you should do now:

Retype the command as **CHKDSK /F**. When asked, type **Y** to convert lost clusters and chains to files.

Error reading drive *x*

See *General failure error reading drive x.*

File cannot be copied onto itself

What happened:

When using the COPY command, you either didn't specify a new path for the file or didn't specify a new name.

What you should do now:

If you typed something like **COPY JENNY.DOC**, DOS didn't know what to do. Copy JENNY.DOC where? If you want to copy the file into the current directory, do you want to give it a new name? Be sure to specify complete paths when copying a file, as in **COPY JENNY.DOC A:** or **COPY JENNY.DOC NEWJENNY.DOC**.

File not found

What happened (1):

You mistyped the file name in the command.

What you should do now:

Retype the command with the correct file name. If necessary, type **DIR /P** to verify the spelling of the file name.

What happened (2):

You mistyped the path leading to the file.

What you should do now:

Verify the path you are using, and make sure that you type a backslash (\) to separate the parts of a path, as in **C:\PROJECTS\DRU\CHAP01.DOC**.

What happened (3):

The file you referenced in the command does not exist.

What you should do now:

Try the command again, with a different file.

General failure error reading drive *x*. Abort, Retry, Fail?

What happened (1):

The diskette in the referenced drive might not be formatted.

What you should do now:

Press **F** for Fail, then format the diskette to its proper density by typing something like **FORMAT A: /V**. See Chapter 13 for more information.

What happened (2):

The diskette in the referenced drive was damaged and could not be read.

What you should do now:

Replace with another diskette and press **R** for Retry, or press **F** for Fail, and reformat this diskette.

What happened (3):

You used the wrong type of diskette, such as a high-density diskette in a double-density drive.

What you should do now:

Reformat the high-density diskette as double-density, or use a diskette of the proper type.

What happened (4):

The diskette in the referenced drive may not be placed in the drive properly.

What you should do now:

Remove the diskette from its drive, and verify that it is placed properly within the drive. If necessary, tap the diskette on the side to make sure that the diskette material has not shifted in the sleeve.

What happened (5):

There is a possibility that the referenced drive is having problems. If you were trying to use the hard disk, this could be the first indicator of some major problems.

What you should do now:

Have a PC guru help you test your hard disk.

What happened (6):

If you were trying to start a program, this could indicate a problem with the program files. If you get this error with a variety of programs, the problem is more likely your hard disk.

What you should do now:

Again, have a PC guru help you test your hard disk. They may recommend re-installing the program.

Insufficient disk space

What happened:

You tried to copy a file onto a diskette, and there was not enough room.

What you should do now:

Delete some files from the diskette to make room for the files you want, or reuse the COPY command with another diskette.

Insufficient memory

What happened:

If you were trying to start a program, and you got this message, you have too many things in memory (RAM), and you need to unload some of them.

What you should do now:

Exit as many programs as possible, then retry the command. If necessary, reboot the computer—rebooting (pressing **Ctrl+Alt+Delete**) causes a computer's memory to clear. You might want to take steps to improve memory usage; see Chapter 19 for more information.

Invalid directory

What happened (1):

You tried to change to a directory that does not exist, or you misspelled the directory name.

What you should do now:

Check the spelling of the directory. If you have at least DOS 5, type **DIR C:*. /S** to display a listing of directories on your hard disk.

What happened (2):

You forgot to place a backslash between a directory and a subdirectory name.

What you should do now:

Remember to use a backslash (\\) to separate the parts of a path name, as in **C:\WORD\DOCS**.

Invalid drive specification

What happened (1):

You referenced a drive that does not exist.

What you should do now:

Type a valid drive letter.

What happened (2):

You referenced a network drive that you are not yet logged onto.

What you should do now:

Log on the network drive, then repeat the original command.

Invalid file name or file not found

What happened (1):

You used the TYPE command with wild cards, as in TYPE *.BAT.

What you should do now:

You can only use the TYPE command on a single file name, as in **TYPE AUTOEXEC.BAT.**

What happened (2):

You tried to rename a file to an invalid file name.

What you should do now:

Try renaming the file to something else. If you need to review the list of valid file names, refer to Chapter 6.

Invalid media or Track 0 Bad

What happened:

You tried to format a diskette to the wrong density, or the diskette was badly damaged.

What you should do now:

Verify the density of the diskette and try formatting it again.

Invalid parameter or Invalid switch

What happened (1):

You used a parameter or switch that is invalid for this command.

What you should do now:

Check the appropriate chapter in this book, and follow the examples carefully.

What happened (2):

You entered a space between the forward slash and the character when entering a switch.

What you should do now:

If you want to enter a switch for a command, such as the /W switch for the DIR command (which tells the DIR command to display files in a wide format), do not type a space between the forward slash (/) and the W. Type the command like this: **DIR /W** and not like this: DIR / W.

What happened (3):

You used a backward slash when specifying a switch.

What you should do now:

Use a forward slash for switches, as in **DIR /W** and not DIR \W.

What happened (4):

You used a forward slash when specifying a file name path.

What you should do now:

Use a backward slash (\) when specifying the path to a file, as in **C:\WORD\NEW.DOC**.

Invalid path

What happened:

You specified an incorrect path to a file, or you mistyped a directory name.

What you should do now:

Verify the path and retype the command.

Invalid path, not directory, or directory not empty

What happened (1):

You used the RD command to remove a directory, and that directory contained subdirectories or files.

What you should do now:

Delete the files and subdirectories first, then repeat the RD command. If you use DOS 6, you can use the DELTREE command instead. See Chapter 12 for more information.

What happened (2):

You used the RD command to remove a directory, and the path you typed was invalid.

What you should do now:

Check the path to the directory you are trying to delete. Remember to use a backslash (\) to separate the parts of a path, as in C:\WORD\DOCS.

Non-system disk or disk error. Replace and strike any key when ready

What happened:

You left a diskette in drive A while you booted the computer.

What you should do now:

Remove the diskette and press **Ctrl+Alt+Delete** at the same time. Do not press "**any key to continue**," as the screen suggests, because you run the risk of transmitting a virus to your system if the diskette is infected.

Not ready reading drive x. Abort, Retry, Fail?

What happened (1):

You typed a command that referenced a diskette drive, and there was no diskette in that drive.

What you should do now:

Place a diskette in the drive, then press **R** for Retry. If you no longer want to execute the command, press **A** for Abort.

What happened (2):

You didn't close the diskette drive door.

What you should do now:

Close the door and press **R** for retry.

Press any key to continue...

What happened:

This is not an error message. DOS is pausing while it waits for you to do something, such as switch diskettes in a drive, or read the display.

What you should do now:

When you are ready to continue, you can press any key on the keyboard, such as the Enter key. Do not look for a key called "Any." Although it sounds as if there should be a specific key you should press, you can actually press any key you want.

Required parameter missing

What happened:

You left out some required part of a command.

What you should do now:

Refer to the appropriate chapter in this book, and follow the examples closely. Also, "A DOS Command Reference That Even My Mother Would Love" includes the most common DOS commands and several examples of how to use them.

Source diskette bad or incompatible

What happened:

When using the DISKCOPY command, you specified two diskette drives of different densities.

What you should do now:

If the two diskette drives are different densities, you'll have to use one drive to do your disk copying, as in **DISKCOPY B: B:**.

Specified drive does not exist or is non-removeable

What happened (1):

When using the DISKCOPY command, you specified a hard disk drive.

What you should do now:

Use only diskette drive letters with the DISKCOPY command, as in **DISKCOPY A: A:**.

What happened (2):

When using the DISKCOPY command, you specified a nonexistent drive.

What you should do now:

Make sure you specify valid drive letters.

Warning: all data on non-removable disk drive *x*: will be lost! Proceed with Format (Y/N)?

What happened:

You used the FORMAT command and did not specify a drive, or you specified a hard disk drive.

What you should do now:

Press **N**, then retype the FORMAT command with a diskette drive specified, as in **FORMAT B:**.

Write protect error writing drive *x*

What happened:

You tried to copy data onto a protected diskette.

What you should do now:

If you really want to do this, remove the write-protect tab (if it's a 5 1/4-inch diskette) or move the write-protect switch to cover the "hole" (if it's a 3 1/2-inch diskette), and then press **R** for Retry. If you don't want to copy the file, press **A** for Abort.

Before You Call the PC Doctor

When your computer starts acting up, there are some easy things you can do. This part of the book contains a list of common situations and their possible solutions.

My Computer's Acting Weird

This is a hard one to nail down, but before you call for help, check these things first:

- ☞ Check the cables and make sure that none of them are loose.

- ☞ Turn the power off, and then back on. Sometimes resetting the computer is all it needs—especially if you leave the power on all the time.

- ☞ Think about what is happening. Do you notice any trends? Ask yourself these questions:

  Does the weirdness start when you use a particular program? If so, reinstalling the program or checking its setup may help.

  Does the weirdness happen when you use the mouse? Are there strange characters on the screen, or does the mouse pointer go where no mouse has gone before? If so, try cleaning your mouse. Open the bottom latch that holds the trackball, and clean all the gook off the rollers. Check the mouse cord to be sure it isn't pinched. Disable the mouse for a few days or borrow one (if it's the same brand) and see if the problems go away—if so, you may need a new mouse.

Has anything changed lately? Have you installed a new program or added any hardware? Did you make any changes to your CONFIG.SYS or AUTOEXEC.BAT files? If you have an old version of the files, try copying it onto your hard disk and see if the problem goes away.

Can you duplicate the error? Is this a one-time thing, or does it happen whenever you do a particular task?

Are you typing too fast? Sometimes an older computer just can't keep up. Try going slower and paying more attention to what you're doing—maybe you're using the wrong commands.

☛ Check for viruses. Most problems have nothing to do with computer viruses, but to be sure, you should check. Refer to Chapter 17 for more information.

☛ There are some disk utilities that you can purchase that can diagnose and even fix most problems with hard disks. Try Norton Utilities, PC Tools, or Mace Utilities.

My Computer Won't Start at All

This one can be real scary, but don't panic until you've checked these things:

☛ Check cables and make sure they are not loose.

☛ Make sure that the computer is getting power. Check the power strip/surge protector; it may need resetting. If necessary, plug a lamp into the socket that the computer normally uses to verify that it works. Most computers make a humming noise when they are on.

☛ Is the monitor on? I can't remember how many times I forget to turn this stupid thing on and begin to panic. If the monitor is on, is it dimmed? Play with the contrast knobs for a while.

☛ Can you boot from a floppy disk? To check, place a system disk in drive A, turn the computer off, and then on again. If your computer starts this way, see the next section.

My Hard Drive's Gone!

If your computer starts okay from a floppy disk but you can't use your hard disk, think about these things:

☞ Have you recently made changes to your AUTOEXEC.BAT or CONFIG.SYS? If so, you may have accidentally deleted commands that load a driver file that the computer uses to initialize a disk drive. These driver files are necessary if you are using a disk compression utility, or if you have a large hard disk (over 32MB) and a DOS version prior to DOS 4. Boot your disk with your emergency diskette, and copy the AUTOEXEC.BAT and CONFIG.SYS files back onto the hard disk.

☞ If you've changed your PC battery or the computer's hardware recently, you may need to run your computer's SETUP program. Get a PC guru to help you.

☞ There are some disk utilities that you can purchase that can diagnose and even fix most problems with hard disks. Try Norton Utilities, PC Tools, or Mace Utilities.

> ### By the Way . . .
> Although I love and use all three of these utilities, the Mace Emergency Room program is my particular favorite; it helped me one time when I thought I'd never see my hard disk again.

My Computer's Locked Up!

This is not a hard one to notice: you're running a program, when suddenly you realize your computer isn't paying any attention to you. Don't bang helplessly on the keyboard! Here are some more productive things you can try:

☞ Try pressing **Esc**. This is the simplest and least damaging thing to do.

☞ If Esc doesn't work, try pressing **Ctrl** and C at the same time (or **Ctrl** and **Break**). This sends a signal to DOS that says, "Hey, I'm here—pay attention to me!"

☞ As a last resort, reboot by pressing **Ctrl+Alt+Delete** at the same time. (If your computer has a reset button, this does basically the same thing, except that sometimes the reset button works when Ctrl+Alt+Del won't.) You can pretty much expect to lose some data with this method. When you get your program started again, check the document you were working on for missing pieces.

By the Way . . .

The easiest way you can recover from problems is to save your document often while you're working on it. Some programs contain an automatic save feature that is quite nice—use it if your program has one. I set mine to save every 10 minutes. That way, I never lose any more than 10 minutes worth of stuff if I have to reboot.

I Just Spilled Something on My Keyboard!

Oops! Follow these steps:

1. Turn everything off.

2. Dab up what you can, using a clean cloth.

3. Let everything dry out. I'd recommend waiting a day before you use the keyboard.

4. Don't spray anything on the keyboard to clean it! This can damage it.

5. If necessary, you can remove the keys to clean underneath them. It's okay; they are built to snap off and on—but be careful.

6. Once everything is working again, don't keep any drinks in the work area. I know, I know—I just can't function without my morning tea—but it's a good idea if you can do it.

I Can't Get Anything to Print

Sometimes getting a new printer to work is hard, but here are some things you can try:

- ☞ Check the cable. Is it loose?

- ☞ Does the printer have power? Can you see lights?

- ☞ Is the printer on-line? Look for a button you can press.

- ☞ Turn the printer off and on to reset it. Sometimes, this is all it needs.

- ☞ Try printing a screen. Exit your program and then press the **Shift** and **Print Screen** keys at the same time.

- ☞ Try printing a file. Exit your program and type this:

    PRINT C:\AUTOEXEC.BAT

    If you see the message **Name of list device [PRN]**, just press **Enter**.

- ☞ Can you print at the DOS prompt, but not in the application? Your printer may not be installed properly for the application. Check the manual (yech) for instructions on how to install a printer.

A DOS Command Reference That Even My Mother Would Love

Most DOS command references are complex, difficult to interpret, and almost impossible to understand unless you've had lots of experience using the command before. This command reference is different; it includes many examples so you can get the command right the first time.

At the beginning of this part of the book, you'll find a guide to the commands you use every day. Other commands that you might be interested in are listed at the end.

Some Things You Should Know Before You Use DOS Commands

Here's a quick review of some important concepts you need to know when working with DOS commands:

Remember to press Enter to execute a command. Until you press Enter, nothing will happen.

DOS commands are tricky. Follow the examples carefully; don't add extra spaces.

A DOS path is what DOS follows to find a file. It's like telling a friend how to find your house. A path name consists of three parts:

☞ The drive the file is located on followed by a colon, as in **C:**.

☛ A backslash (\) followed by the complete path to the file. Start with the parent directory. Then add another backslash, and a subdirectory name, if applicable. Finish up with a final backslash, as in **\PROJECTS\RESTOFUS**.

☛ End the path name with a file name or file specification, as in **CHAPTR08.DOC**.

The completed path would look like this:

C:\PROJECTS\RESTOFUS\CHAPTR08.DOC

You can use DOS wild cards to specify more than one file to use in a single command:

☛ **The asterisk (*)** represents several characters within a file name. For example, *.DOC means "use files that have any first name, but a last name of DOC."

☛ **The question mark (?)** represents a single character within a file name. For example, JO?N.WK1 means "use files that begin with the letters JO, followed by any character, followed by an N, and the extension .WK1."

The most common error message you get when using DOS commands is Bad command or file name.   If you get this error message, you need to set up a DOS path so that DOS can find the command. See Chapter 4 for more details.

DOS Commands You'll Really Use

You'll use the DOS commands in this section every day as you go about your business, which you'll get back to even sooner with these easy-to-follow examples.

CD (CHDIR)

Displays the current directory.

Example: CD

Changes to a different directory.

Examples: CD\WORD

CD\WORD\DOCS

What you should know: If you type just CD, DOS will display the name of the directory you are currently in. To change to a different directory, type CD\ followed by the name of the directory to change to.

Where to go for more help: Chapters 6 and 12

CHKDSK

Displays available disk and memory space and corrects disk errors.

Example: CHKDSK C: /F

What you should know: Use CHKDSK periodically to check your hard disk for lost clusters and chains. Lost clusters and chains are caused when DOS does not properly update its file tracking system. DOS is sometimes a very bad housekeeper, so lost clusters and chains are normal; they are nothing to be afraid of. If CHKDSK converts lost clusters or chains to files, then use this command:

DEL C:\FILE????.CHK

Where to go for more help: Chapter 19

CLS

Use anytime you want to clear your screen.

Example: CLS

COPY

Makes a copy (duplicate) of a file or files.

Example: COPY AUTOEXEC.BAT AUTOEXEC.BAK

Places a copy of a file in a different directory or disk.

Examples: COPY C:\MKTG\SALES93.WKS D:\SALES

COPY C:\AUTOEXEC.BAT A:

COPY A:*.* C:\PROJECTS

COPY C:\WORD\OLDFILE.DOC C:\PROJECTS\NEWFILE.DOC

What you should know: The first part of the COPY command tells DOS the name (and directory path) of the file(s) to copy. The second part of the COPY command tells DOS the name of the drive or directory to copy the file to (along with a new name for the file if you want). You can leave off part of the command if you happen to be in the directory that you are copying *from* or *to*, but that is generally confusing, so you're better off typing entire directory paths. Also, you can use DOS wild cards to specify more than one file to copy.

Where to go for more help: Chapter 10

DEL

Deletes a file or files.

Examples: DEL OLDFILE.DOC

DEL *.* /P

What you should know: If you have at least DOS 4, you can add /P to the end of the DEL command to be prompted before a file is deleted. You can also use wild cards with the DEL command to delete more than one file at a time.

Where to go for more help: Chapter 11

DELTREE (To use, you need DOS 6)

Deletes a directory and its subdirectories without having to remove the files first.

Examples: DELTREE C:\SALES92

DELTREE C:\PROJECTS\DRU

What you should know: You can not undelete files if you also delete the directory they were in.

Where to go for more help: Chapter 12

DIR

Lists files in the specified directory or drive.

Examples: DIR /P   (one screen at a time)

DIR A: (list files on drive A)

DIR /W   (list files across the screen)

Lists files in a specific order (you need at least DOS 5).

Examples: DIR /O:E (sorted by extension or type)

DIR /O:D (sorted by date)

DIR /O:S   (sorted by size)

Finds specific files (you need at least DOS 5).

Examples: DIR C:\LOST.DOC /S

DIR C:*.BAK /S

What you should know: You can use DOS wild cards to list specific files. Also, you can sort files in reverse order by typing a minus in front of the sort letter, as in -D.

Where to go for more help: Chapter 9

DISKCOPY

Makes a copy of a diskette.

Examples: DISKCOPY A: A:

DISKCOPY A: B:

What you should know: The first drive letter tells the location of the original, or source diskette. The second drive letter tells the location of the target diskette. Both drives must be the same size and density. If you have to use a single drive (like drive A), you'll be prompted when to switch disks back and forth. Start with the source disk in the drive.

Where to go for more help: Chapter 13

DOSSHELL (To use, you need at least DOS 4)

Starts the DOS Shell.

Example: DOSSHELL

What you should know: The DOS Shell is a graphical interface that allows you to perform common DOS tasks by selecting icons (pictures) instead of typing commands. The DOS Shell is easy to use and great for beginners.

Where to go for more help: Chapter 7

EDIT (To use, you need at least DOS 5)

Creates or edits a text or a batch file.

Examples: EDIT C:\AUTOEXEC.BAT

EDIT NEWFILE.TXT

What you should know: EDIT is a simple editor that you can use to edit your CONFIG.SYS or AUTOEXEC.BAT files, or to create simple batch files of your own.

Where to go for more help: Chapter 16

EDLIN

Creates or edits a text or batch file.

Examples: EDLIN C:\AUTOEXEC.BAT

EDLIN NEWFILE.TXT

What you should know: EDLIN is a simple editor that you can use to edit your CONFIG.SYS or AUTOEXEC.BAT files, or to create simple batch files of your own. Use EDIT instead of EDLIN if you have at least DOS 5.

Where to go for more help: Chapter 16

EXIT

Returns to your application after using its DOS shell to access the DOS command prompt.

Example: EXIT

What you should know: A temporary command prompt allows you access to the DOS prompt without having to exit an application. For example, you can type a letter, use the DOS Shell to format a diskette, then return to the application and save the file.

Where to go for more help: Chapter 21

FORMAT

Prepares a diskette for use.

Example: FORMAT A: /V

When to use: To create an emergency diskette.

Example: FORMAT A: /S /V

Formats a double-density diskette in a high-density drive, using at least DOS 4.

Examples: FORMAT A: /F:360   (5 1/4-inch)

FORMAT A: /F:720   (3 1/2-inch)

Formats a double-density diskette in a high-density drive, using a DOS version prior to 4.

Examples: FORMAT A: /4   (5 1/4-inch)

FORMAT A: /N:9 /T:80   (3 1/2-inch)

Reformats a diskette that had been formatted previously, using at least DOS 5.

Example: FORMAT B: /Q

Formats a diskette unconditionally, using at least DOS 5.

Example: FORMAT B: /U

What you should know: You must format a diskette in order to use it the first time. Be sure to type the drive letter to format, and use only drives A and B. If you have at least DOS 5, you can unformat a diskette by using the UNFORMAT command.

Where to go for more help: Chapter 13

HELP (To use, you need at least DOS 5)

Accesses the DOS help system.

Example: HELP FORMAT

What you should know: You can also type /? after a command to get help with syntax, as in FORMAT /?.

Where to go for more help: Chapter 8

MD (MKDIR)

Creates a directory.

Examples: MD C:\WORD\DOCS

MD TEMP

What you should know: MD will create a subdirectory of the current directory unless you specify a directory path.

Where to go for more help: Chapter 12

MOVE (To use, you need DOS 6)

Moves a file to a different location.

Examples: MOVE C:\TAXES\93BUDGET.WKS D:\NEW

MOVE C:\WORD*.DOC C:\LETTERS

Renames a directory.

Example: MOVE C:\OLDDIR C:\NEWDIR

What you should know: You can move more than one file at a time by using DOS wild cards.

Where to go for more help: Chapter 10

RD (RMDIR)

Removes a directory if it's empty of files.

Example: RD \PROGRAMS\JUNK

What you should know: Use the DEL command to remove its files, then use RD to remove a directory. If you have DOS 6, you can remove directories in one step by using the DELTREE command.

Where to go for help: Chapter 12

REN

Renames a file.

Examples: REN OLDFILE.DOC NEWFILE.DOC

REN 92*.WKS 93*.WKS

What you should know: You can't rename a file to the same name that another file is using; no two files in the same directory can have the same name. You can rename more than one file at a time by using DOS wild cards. If you want to rename a directory and you have DOS 6, see the MOVE command.

Where to go for help: Chapter 10

TYPE

Displays the contents of a text or a batch file.

Example: TYPE C:\AUTOEXEC.BAT | MORE

What you should know: Always include the | **MORE** filter with the TYPE command, or the contents of the file may scroll off the screen. Don't use the TYPE command on a program file (such as a file with an .EXE or a .COM extension) because all you'll get is a bunch of beeps and some weird characters.

Where to go for more help: Chapter 9

UNDELETE (To use, you need at least DOS 5)

Restores an accidentally deleted file.

Example: UNDELETE C:\WORD\IMPTFILE.DOC

What you should know: Always try to undelete a file as soon as possible. Do not copy or create new files until you've recovered your lost file. Your chances of recovering a lost file are better if you establish a delete tracking system.

Where to go for more help: Chapter 11

UNFORMAT (To use, you need at least DOS 5)

Unformats an accidentally formatted disk.

Example: UNFORMAT A:

What you should know: If a disk was formatted with the /U switch, it cannot be unformatted.

Where to go for more help: Chapter 13

VER

Displays the current DOS version.

Example: VER

What you should know: Many DOS commands are only available on recent versions of DOS. Use this command to determine the DOS version your PC uses.

Where to go for more help: Chapter 2

DOS Commands You'll Use Occasionally

Here are some less common commands that you may need now and then. Don't worry about learning them until you actually need them.

Command	What to use it for	Where to get more help
BACKUP	Saves duplicates of files as insurance against damage	Chapter 14
DATE	Enters or changes the system date	Chapter 3
DBLSPACE	Compresses disks	Chapter 18
DOSKEY	Recalls previous commands	Chapter 4
MEM	Checks memory usage	Chapter 19
MEMMAKER	Configures memory usage	Chapter 19
MIRROR	Enables delete protection	Chapter 19
MSAV	Protects against computer viruses	Chapter 17
MSBACKUP	Saves duplicates of files as insurance against damage	Chapter 14
PROMPT	Changes the system prompt	Chapter 6
RESTORE	Restores duplicates of files if originals become damaged	Chapter 15
TIME	Enters or changes system time	Chapter 3
TREE	Displays a listing of directories	Chapter 12
VOL	Displays the volume label of a drive	Chapter 13
VSAFE	Protects against computer viruses	Chapter 17

Glossary

Speak Like a Geek: The Complete Archives

The computer world is like an exclusive club complete with its own language. If you want to be accepted, you need to learn the lingo (the secret handshake comes later). The following mini-glossary will help you get started.

application   (1) The placement of shampoo on the head. (2) Also known as *program*, a set of instructions that enable a computer to perform a specific task, such as word processing or data management.

ASCII file   A file containing characters that can be used by any program on any computer. Sometimes called a *text file* or an *ASCII text file*. (ASCII is pronounced "ASK-key.")

AUTOEXEC.BAT   A special file that contains commands that are automatically executed when your computer is booted.

backing up   (1) The movement of my car when parked on a hill. (2) A process that copies your files onto diskettes in a special compressed format. If something bad happens to the originals, you can restore your backed-up files (a process that uncompresses the files and copies them back).

batch file   A batch file ends in .BAT and contains a number of commands batched together in one file. You create batch files to perform several commands in sequence for you.

BIOS (basic input-output system)   The BIOS controls input/ouput between the various elements that make up the computer, including disk drives, the printer, the ports, and the monitor.

bits   Binary digits. Each bit is like a light switch: it's either ON (1) or OFF (0). Place eight bits in a row, and you form a byte, or a pattern that represents a single character, such as the letter J.

boot   (1) What you really feel like doing to a computer that refuses to understand. (2) The process of starting a computer. The word *booting* comes from the phrase, "pulling yourself up by the bootstraps," which basically describes what happens when a computer starts: first it gets power, then it checks itself out, then it loads DOS and awaits your command.

boot drive   Your boot drive is the drive that contains your operating system files, usually drive C.

burn-in   (1) What happens to my skin no matter how much suntan lotion I use. (2) Burn-in happens when the same image is displayed too long on a PC monitor. When other images are shown, the burned-in image is still there, like a ghost on the screen.

byte   A byte is the amount of space it takes to store a character, such as 1, Q, or $. A byte is made up of eight *bits*; for example, the byte 01000001 represents the letter A.

capacity   A measure of how much data a disk can store. For example, a 5 1/4-inch, high-density floppy disk can be formatted to store 1.2MB; 1.2MB is the disk's *capacity*.

CD-ROM (compact-disk read-only memory)   A popular add-on for computers is a CD-ROM drive. With a CD-ROM drive, your computer can play ordinary CDs (music) and special computer CDs that store large complex programs or massive amounts of data. A single disk can store over 600MB of information. Pronounced "see-dee-RAHM."

click   To move the mouse pointer over an object or an icon and press and release the mouse button once without moving the mouse.

CMOS (Complementary Metal-Oxide Semiconductor)   (1) That slimy stuff you find on rocks at the beach. (2) Pronounced "SEA-moss," CMOS is an electronic device (usually battery operated) that stores information about your computer. Information stored in CMOS includes the current date and time, and the number and types of disk drives your computer has.

cold boot   Same thing as booting; the process of starting a computer by turning the power on.

command   An order that tells the computer what to do.

communications software   A set of instructions that allows a computer (equipped with the necessary hardware, such as a modem) to communicate with other computers through the telephone lines.

compressed drive   A drive whose storage capacity has increased because of a special program that uses a more effective method (than just DOS alone) of managing disk space.

compression ratio   The proportion of space a file uses on a newly *compressed drive*, as compared to the amount of space it used before the drive was compressed. A compression ratio of 2:1 is optimal.

computer   (1) A hole on my desk into which I throw money. (2) Any machine that accepts input (from a user), processes the input, and produces output in some form.

CONFIG.SYS   A file that customizes your PC for the specific programs that you use by changing the system default values for certain parameters. The commands in the CONFIG.SYS file are executed automatically at system startup.

conventional memory   The working area of the computer, or its "desktop." This is the part of RAM below 640K. Conventional memory is the most important memory because it's the only area of memory in which a program can run. It is the area of memory that DOS uses to manipulate data, run programs, and perform its tasks.

CPU (Central Processing Unit)   See *microprocessor*.

crash   (1) A sound you don't want to hear when you're moving your computer. (2) Failure of a system or program. Usually, you realize that your system has crashed when the display or keyboard locks up. The term *crash* also refers to a disk crash or head crash, which occurs when the read/write head in the disk drive falls on the disk. This would be like dropping a phonograph needle on a record. A disk crash can destroy any data stored where the read/write head fell on the disk.

cursor   A horizontal line that appears below characters. A cursor acts like the tip of your pencil; anything you type appears at the cursor.

data   (1) That guy on Star Trek: The Next Generation. (2) A computer term for information. You enter facts and figures (data) into a computer that then processes it and displays it in an organized manner. In common usage, *data* and *information* are used interchangeably.

data files   See *files*.

database   A type of computer program used for storing, organizing, and retrieving information. Popular database programs include dBASE, Paradox, and Q&A.

defragmentation   (1) What happens when you pull a sweater at one end. (2) When a file is copied onto a drive, parts of the file may be split over different sections of the drive in order to make the most effective use of available space. On an uncompressed drive, fragmentation can cause a drop in speed when accessing files. Defragmenting a drive causes the parts of files that were split up to be placed together.

density   A measure of the amount of data that can be stored per square inch of storage area on a disk. To understand density, think of a disk covered with magnetic dust. Each particle of dust stores one piece of data. No matter how large or small the particle, it still stores only one piece of data. With double-density disks, the particles are large, so the disk can hold fewer particles (less data). With high-density disks, the particles are small, so more particles can be packed in less space, and the disk can store more data.

desktop publishing (DTP)   A program that allows you to combine text and graphics on the same page and manipulate the text and graphics on-screen. Desktop publishing programs are commonly used to create news-letters, brochures, flyers, resumes, and business cards.

dialog box   A dialog box is a special window or box that appears when the program requires additional information before executing a command.

differential backup   A type of backup that copies the files that have been changed since the last full backup. To restore a complete hard disk, you would need *both your full and your differential backup diskettes.*

directory   Because large hard disks can store thousands of files, you often need to store related files in separate directories on the disk. Think of your disk as a filing cabinet and think of each directory as a drawer in the filing cabinet. By keeping files in separate directories, it is easier to locate and work with related files.

disk   A magnetic computer storage medium. See *floppy disk* and *hard disk.*

disk drive   (1) A street in Silicon Valley. (2) A device that writes data to a magnetic disk and reads data from the disk. Think of a disk drive as a cassette recorder/player. Just as the cassette player can record sounds on a magnetic cassette tape and play back those sounds, a disk drive can record data on a magnetic disk and play back that data.

diskette   Another name for *floppy disk.*

document   Any work you create using an application program and save in a file on disk. Although the term *document* traditionally refers to work created in a word processing program, such as a letter or a chapter of a book, *document* is now loosely used to refer to any work, including spread-sheets and databases.

DOS (disk operating system)   DOS, which rhymes with "boss," is an essential program that provides the necessary instructions for the computer's parts to function as a unit (keyboard, disk drive, central pro-cessing unit, display screen, printer, and so on). DOS interprets the com-mands you give your computer. Like a traffic cop, DOS controls the flow of information to each computer component.

DOS prompt   An on-screen prompt that indicates DOS is ready to accept a command. It looks something like **C>** or **C:**.

DOS Shell   The DOS Shell is a graphical interface that keeps you safe and warm, miles away from the nasty world of the DOS prompt. Inside the Shell, you can perform the same commands that you could outside the Shell, but with greater ease (and understanding).

double-click   To move the mouse pointer over an object or icon, and press and release the mouse button twice in quick succession.

drag   (1) Losing a winning lottery ticket. (2) To drag the mouse, first move the mouse to the starting position. Now click and hold the mouse button. Drag the mouse to the ending position, and then release the mouse button.

drivers   Special programs that tell your computer how to communicate with certain devices, such as a mouse.

EMS (expanded memory specification)   See *expanded memory*.

environment   An *environment* is a setting in which you perform tasks on your computer. The DOS Shell, for example, uses a graphical environment that lets you enter commands by selecting pictures rather than by typing commands. This makes it much easier to use your computer (assuming you know what the pictures stand for).

environment area   A part of RAM that acts like a tiny universal notepad. DOS stores information about your prompt, the location of the command interpreter, and your search path in the environment area. Programs use the environment area so their users can customize how that program starts or where important files are to be placed.

executable file   A program file that can run the program. Executable files end in .BAT, .COM, or .EXE.

expanded memory   A special kind of computer memory that is located on an expanded memory board or converted from extended memory. This type of memory cannot be used to run a program, but it can be used by programs for the temporary storage of their data. See also *extended memory*.

extended memory   Extended memory is the part of RAM above 1MB. Extended memory cannot be used to run programs, but can be used by programs to store their data temporarily. If needed, you can customize a portion of extended memory to act like expanded memory for use with programs that can use only expanded memory. See also *expanded memory*.

extension   In DOS, each file you create has a unique name. The name consists of two parts: a file name and an extension. The file name can be up to eight characters. The extension (which is optional) can be up to three characters. The extension normally denotes the file type.

file   (1) What every prisoner wants to find in their birthday cake. (2) DOS stores information in files. Anything can be placed in a file: a memo, a budget report, or even a graphics image (like a picture of a boat or a computer). Files you create are called *data files*. Applications (like a word processing program, with which you can type letters and reports) are composed of several files called *program files*.

file allocation table (FAT)   (1) How I feel after Thanksgiving dinner. (2) A map on every disk that tells the operating system where the files on the disk are stored. It's sort of like a classroom seating chart.

fixed disk drive   A disk drive that has a nonremovable disk, as opposed to floppy disk drives, in which you can insert and remove disks. See also *disk drive*.

floppy disk drive   A disk drive that uses floppy disks. See also *disk drive*.

floppy disks   Small, portable, plastic storage squares that magnetically store *data* (the facts and figures you enter and save). Floppy disks are inserted into your computer's *floppy disk drive* (located on the front of the computer).

formatting   A process that prepares a diskette for use. Formatting creates invisible *tracks* (circles) and *sectors* (pie-shaped wedges) on the surface of the diskette, creating a "map" that DOS can use for keeping track of where files are stored. The number of tracks and sectors that a diskette is divided into determines how much information it can store.

full backup   A type of back up that copies every file on your hard disk.

function keys   The 10 or 12 F keys on the left side of the keyboard or 12 F keys at the top of the keyboard. F keys are numbered F1, F2, F3, and so on. These keys are used to enter various commands in a program.

graphical user interface (GUI, pronounced "goo-ey")   (1) Tar on a hot day. (2) A type of program interface that uses graphical elements, such as icons, to represent commands, files, and (in some cases) other programs. The most *popular* GUI is Microsoft Windows.

graphics/charting program   A program that takes columnar data and creates a professional-looking chart.

graphics mode   A display mode that uses pictures in its display, rather than just text and simple lines. Graphics mode makes the display attractive, but not all monitors and video cards support it.

hard disk   A nonremovable disk drive that stores many megabytes of data. Because it is fixed inside the computer (see *fixed disk drive*), it performs quicker and more efficiently than a floppy disk.

hardware   The physical parts of a computer (such as the *monitor*, the *disk drives*, the *CPU*, and so on). The programs you run are electronic, rather than physical; they're known as *software*.

icon   A graphic image that represents another object, such as a file on a disk.

incremental backup   A type of backup that copies only the files that have been changed since the last full or incremental backup. To restore a complete hard disk, you would need *both your full and all of your incremental backup diskettes*.

initialize   To reset a computer or program to some starting values. When used to describe floppy or hard disks, the term means the same as *format*.

input   Data that goes into your computer. When you press a key or click a mouse button, you are giving your computer input. Data that your computer gives back to you (by printing it out or displaying it on the monitor) is called *output*.

Insert mode   The default typing mode for most word processors and text editors. Insert mode means that when you position your cursor and start to type, what you type is inserted at that point.

jump term   (1) A word that emits a small electrical charge when you use it. (2) A highlighted term in the DOS 6 help system that, when selected, "jumps" to a related section of the help system.

keyboard   The main input device for most computers. The keyboard contains the standard keys that you find on most typewriters, plus a few more.

kilobyte   A unit for measuring the amount of data. A kilobyte (K) is equivalent to 1,024 bytes.

load   To read data or program instructions from disk and place them in the computer's memory, where the computer can use the data or instructions. You usually load a program before you use it or load a file before you edit it.

logical drive   (1) The type of drive that Spock would love. (2) A section of a hard disk or memory that is treated as a separate disk and is assigned its own letter. For example, you may *partition* your hard drive into logical drives C, D, E, and F. It's still one disk, but it is partitioned into logical drives.

lost clusters and lost chains   (1) These are probably with my other sock. (2) Lost clusters and chains are pieces of files that have been "lost" by DOS. When you delete a file, it is not actually erased; instead, the reference to the file's location is erased. If a file's location is erased from the file listing, but its address is still marked "used," you get a lost cluster. You can also get a lost cluster if you reboot while a file is being written to disk. If several of these clusters occur together on the disk, you get a lost chain.

megabyte   A standard unit used to measure the storage capacity of a disk and the amount of computer memory. A megabyte is 1,048,576 bytes (1000 kilobytes). This is roughly equivalent to 500 pages of double-spaced text. Megabyte is commonly abbreviated as MB, M, or Mbyte.

memory   Electronic storage area inside the computer, used to temporarily store data or program instructions when the computer is using them. The computer's memory is erased when the power to the computer is turned off.

menu   A list of commands or instructions displayed on the screen. Menus organize commands and make a program easier to use.

microprocessor   Sometimes called the central processing unit (CPU) or processor, this chip is the computer's brain; it does all the calculations for the computer.

modem   An acronym for MOdulator/DEModulator. A modem lets a computer send and receive data through an ordinary telephone line.

monitor   A television-like screen that the computer uses to display information.

mouse   (1) The last name of a little guy named Mickey. (2) A mouse is a device that moves an arrow (a pointer) on the screen. When you move the mouse, the pointer on the screen moves in the same direction. Used instead of the keyboard to select and move items (such as text or graphics), execute commands, and perform other tasks. A mouse gets its name because it connects to your computer through a long "tail" or cord.

MS-DOS (Microsoft Disk Operating System)   See *DOS*.

multitasking   (1) What you should not do while driving a car. (2) The capability to run two programs at the same time. Some programs, such as the DOS Shell, allow you to switch between two or more programs but do not allow a program to perform operations in the background. This is called *task-switching*, not multitasking.

network   Connecting several PCs together for the purpose of sharing information and printers. In a local area network (LAN), the connected PCs are located in the same building. In a wide area network (WAN), the connected PCs can be located thousands of miles apart.

output   Data (computer information) that your computer gives back to you. Output can be displayed on a computer's monitor, stored on disk, or printed on the printer. Output is the opposite of *input*, which is the data that you enter into the computer.

Overtype mode   The opposite of *Insert mode*, as used in word processors and text editors. Overtype mode means that when you position your cursor and start to type, what you type replaces existing characters at that point.

parameter   A part of a DOS command that tells it which files, directories, or drives to work with.

partition   A hard disk drive can be divided (or *partitioned*) into one or more drives, which DOS refers to as drive C, drive D, drive E, and so on. (Don't be fooled; it's still one disk drive.) The actual hard disk drive is called the *physical* drive; each partition is called a *logical* drive.

path   The route that DOS travels from the root directory to any subdirectories when locating a file. Think of telling a friend how to find your house. A complete path looks like this: C:\WORD\DOCS\CHAP01.DOC.

PC   See *personal computer*.

peripheral   The system unit is the central part of the computer. Any devices that are attached to the system unit are considered *peripheral* (as in peripheral vision). Peripheral devices include the monitor, printer, keyboard, mouse, modem, and joystick. Some manufacturers consider the keyboard and monitor as essential parts of the computer rather than as peripherals.

personal computer   A personal computer (or PC for short) is a machine that is small enough to fit on a desktop and is intended to be used by an individual to perform daily tasks, such as typing, calculating, organizing, and filing.

personal finance program   Personal finance programs are often called *check-writing* programs, because their main purpose is to help you keep a balanced checkbook. However, these programs are becoming more diverse. Some personal finance programs can be used to manage the finances of a small business, and others (such as Wealth Starter) contain tools for teaching you how to invest your money intelligently.

pie chart   A type of chart shaped like a circle that is divided into pieces, like a pie. Each item that's charted (such as AT&T, MCI, and Sprint) is given a "pie piece" that represents their portion of the whole circle.

pipe character   The character (|) that controls the flow of information between two DOS commands, as in **TYPE AUTOEXEC.BAT | MORE**.

ports   The receptacles at the back of the computer. They get their name from the ports where ships pick up and deliver cargo. In this case, the ports allow information to enter and leave the system unit.

POST (Power-On Self Test)   (1) The part that holds up a fence.
(2) A series of internal checks the computer performs on itself whenever it is booted. If the test reveals that any component is not working properly, the computer displays an error message on-screen giving a general indication of which component is causing problems.

printer   Most computers have a printer for printing copies of your data. The data that comes out of your computer is called *output*.

program   A set of instructions written in a special "machine language" that the computer understands. Typical programs are word processors, spreadsheets, databases, and games.

program files   See *files*.

prompt   A message from DOS letting you know that it is waiting for a command. When you type a command, it appears next to the prompt on the screen. Typical DOS prompts include **C>** or **C:\DOS>**.

pull-down menu   Contains the selections for a main menu command. This type of menu, when activated, is pulled down below the main menu bar, like a window shade can be pulled down from the top of a window frame.

random-access memory (RAM)   A temporary electronic storage, where your computer keeps data that it is working with. Any information that the computer needs to use (data, programs, even DOS commands) must be placed in RAM so the computer can access them. The computer forgets everything in its memory when you turn the computer off, so you need a means of permanently storing data you want to keep: either on a hard disk or on a floppy diskette.

rebooting   The process of restarting a computer that is already on. Press Ctrl+Alt+Delete to reboot. Also known as *warm booting*.

redirection symbol   Used in a command to send the output of that command to another device, a file, or another command, instead of displaying the output on the monitor. The DOS redirection symbol is the greater-than sign (>), and it is by the the name of the device, the file, or the command you want to direct the output to, like this: **DIR > PRN**.

restoring files   Backing up your files is a process that copies files onto diskettes in a special compressed format. If those files get damaged somehow, you can restore them through a reverse process that decompresses the backed-up files and copies them back.

ROM BIOS   See *BIOS*.

root directory   The main, or central, directory. All other directories branch off from the root.

scroll   To move text up/down or right/left on a computer screen.

shell   (1) What Sue sells by the seashore. (2) A program that lets you choose operating system commands by choosing from a menu. Shell programs make the operating system easier to use.

software   Any instructions that tell your computer (the *hardware*) what to do. There are two types of software: operating system software and application software. Operating system software (such as *DOS*) gets your computer up and running. *Application* software allows you to do something useful, such as type a letter or save the whales.

spreadsheet   A computer program that organizes information in columns and rows and performs calculations. If you want to balance a checkbook or last year's budget, use a spreadsheet program.

subdirectories   Means the same thing as directories. The prefix *sub* is used to emphasize the fact that all directories are subordinate to the root directory. Sometimes, the word *subdirectories* is used to describe a directory under another directory.

surge protector/power strip   A special kind of power strip that protects your PC against sudden power surges.

switch   (1) A pretty good movie starring Ellen Barkin. (2) The part of a DOS command that modifies the way in which the command is carried out. Switches are always preceded with a forward slash (/). For example, the DIR command has a switch (/W) that lists files going across the screen instead of down.

temporary DOS prompt   A special part of a regular application that allows the user to perform needed file maintenance functions without actually exiting an application.

text file   A type of file that contains no special formatting (such as bold), but simply letters, numbers, and such.

text mode   A display mode that uses text and simple lines or boxes, rather than pictures. Text mode can be used with almost any monitor and video card and is especially useful for those that do not support graphics.

TSR (terminate and stay resident)   Special programs that start and then "go to sleep" until they are reactivated by a special key combination.

uninterruptible power supply (UPS)   A battery-powered device that protects against power spikes and power outages. If the power goes out, the UPS continues supplying power to the computer so you can continue working or safely turn off your computer without losing any data.

upper memory   The area of RAM between 640K and 1MB. This area is reserved for DOS.

video card   A circuit board in your computer that works with your *monitor* to project images on your screen.

virus   A computer virus is a program that vandalizes your system. The worst viruses destroy data and render your computer helpless. Others display strange messages, but do no damage. A virus can enter your system through an infected diskette or an infected file that has been downloaded (received through a modem) from another computer.

volume label   A brief description or name for a disk, recorded electronically on the disk itself during the format process. A volume label displays when DIR is used to list the files on the disk.

warm boot   See *rebooting*.

wild card   A wild card is used to represent characters within a file name. Wild cards create a general file name pattern so that several files can be used with a single DOS command. There are two DOS wild cards: the asterisk (*), which represents several characters within a file name, and the question mark (?), which represents a single character. Think of a wild-card character as a wild card in a game of poker. If the Joker is wild, you can use it in place of any card in the entire deck of cards.

windows   (1) Something I don't do. (2) A box that is used to display information in part of the screen. Often used as a nickname for Microsoft Windows, a graphical interface program (see *GUI*).

word processor   A program that lets you enter, edit, format, and print text. Used for typing letters, reports, envelopes, and other tasks that would normally require a typewriter.

write-protect   To prevent a computer from adding or modifying data stored on a disk.

Index

E

F

G

H

I

N

Q

T

W

X-Z